The Gateway to Global Payroll

Orange Books Publication

1st Floor, Rajhans Arcade, Mall Road, Kohka, Bhilai, Chhattisgarh 490020

Website: **www.orangebooks.in**

© Copyright, 2024, Author

All rights reserved. No part of this book may be reproduced, stored in a retrieval system, or transmitted, in any form by any means, electronic, mechanical, magnetic, optical, chemical, manual, photocopying, recording or otherwise, without the prior written consent of its writer.

First Edition, 2024

ISBN: 978-93-6554-715-3

THE GATEWAY TO
GLOBAL PAYROLL

HARES ANANTH KUMARESSAN & NIDHI SOLANKI

Orange Books Publication
www.orangebooks.in

About the Authors

Like many engineers of the 21st century, I (Hares Ananth) began my career in a Human Resource Outsourcing (HRO) organization after completing my degree in Automobile Engineering in 2011 ☺. I worked diligently, developed a passion for my work, and grew to love global payroll. I was fortunate to gain experience across various domains, including vendor management, implementation, operations, product management, integration, customer success, and product marketing. It has been an incredible journey, and this diversity is what global payroll offers.

Nidhi Solanki joined the company when I was focused on implementation. Together, in 2013, we built simple solutions for complex payroll problems. We started by creating payroll calculators in spreadsheets, studying income tax and social security rules from countries we knew to those we have not heard of before. Within months we were talking to engineers and building global Payroll solutions and products. Nidhi has since continued her work in payroll implementation, operations, and global compliance advisory teams.

Why Are We Writing This Book?

We love our work and recognized the need for a structured approach to prepare fresh graduates for the rapidly growing billion-dollar global payroll market. This book aims to equip college graduates with the knowledge and skills necessary to be hired by a global payroll organization. Our goal is to make you fall in love with payroll and set you on a journey in this industry. Trust us, once you start, the sky's the limit in this field.

Authors Acknowledgement

It takes a village to raise a child, and it takes a small army to write a book. This book is no different. A talented group of people made this book possible.

This book is a testament to the collective wisdom of countless individuals who've navigated the labyrinth of payroll. We owe a debt of gratitude to the pioneers who transformed ancient barter systems into the complex world of modern payroll. A special thanks to our colleagues, mentors, and friends who've shared their knowledge and experiences.

Mr. Guhan Ramanan, who taught me that once you can write the problem statement clearly, half the problem is solved. Special thanks to Mr. Ashok Bildiker, a visionary who trusted me and spent his valuable time with me, showing that while problems can be complex, solutions should be simple. My first managers, Mr. Shakil Gour and Priyankan, treated me like their younger brother and taught me everything from how to open a spreadsheet to how to be a good leader, and I am grateful for giving me the freedom. Shravan Kumar Manthena – thank you for teaching me work ethics and the importance of not shying away from making your hands dirty in work regardless of who or what you do and making decisions with integrity.

I am grateful to Balamalai, a wonderful person, who gave hope, when I badly needed it, and to Shankar Sir, my brilliant neighbor, who shares valuable life lessons with a freshly brewed coffee every day! Both the coffee and the lessons are priceless. Thanks for the initial proofreading and supporting the idea of writing this book.

And most importantly, I would like to thank Nidhi Solanki, who was just as enthusiastic and daring as I was to embark on this adventurous journey of writing this book. Without her partnership and dedication, this project would not have been possible. Finally, thanks to my great friend Raakesh Mohan, who is always there for me, my wife Bharthi, who supported me throughout the entire process, and my dad, A. Kumaressan, my first friend and the best guru I could ever ask for.

We're also indebted to the unsung heroes of the payroll world - the number crunchers, the policy wonks, Payroll processors, Implementation specialists, Product Managers and the software engineers who make it all possible. And, of course, to our families and friends who endured our payroll rants with unwavering support.

Last but not least, a nod to the digital overlords, Gemini and ChatGPT, for their tireless assistance in transforming our thoughts into words.

How to Read This Book

For Payroll Novices:

If you're new to the world of payroll, this book is designed to be your friendly guide. Start from the beginning and enjoy the journey through the history and evolution of payroll. Each chapter builds upon the previous, so a sequential reading is recommended.

For Payroll Professionals:

Feel free to dive into specific sections based on your interests or areas of expertise. The book is structured to allow for flexibility, so you can use it as a reference guide or to explore new topics. The practical examples and insights can be valuable for both beginners and experienced professionals.

For Everyone:

- Engage with the content: The book is written in an engaging and informative style, making it easy to follow and understand.
- Explore the examples: The practical examples and case studies will help you apply the concepts to real-world scenarios.
- Use the book as a resource: Refer back to specific sections as needed for quick reference or further exploration.

Remember: Payroll is a dynamic field, so continuous learning is essential. This book is a starting point on your payroll journey.

Content

The Payroll Pilgrim: A Worldwide Quest 1
   Introduction 2
   Will you like What you will do? 4
   Will Payroll Keep You Hooked for the Long Haul? 4
   Internal Payroll vs. Payroll Service Provider 5
   The Beauty of Payroll: A Flexible Career Path! 6

Basics of Payroll Process 9
   Payroll Terminologies 9
   Stages of Payroll 19
   Feeding the Payroll Machine: Uploading the Data 22
   Common Challenges 29
   The Post-Payroll Stage 31
   Delivering the Pay 31
   Fulfilling Statutory Obligations 31
   Internal Reporting and Accounting 31
   Bank File: Enabling Smooth Payments 32
   GL File: Feeding the Financial Engine 33
   Key Considerations 33
   Post-Payroll: The Importance of Employee Query Resolution 35
   Understanding the Critical Role of Query Resolution 35
   Query Classification and Resolution 36
   The Importance of Human Touch 36
   Key Considerations for Effective Query Resolution 37
   Common Challenges 37
   Best Practices 37
   Building Blocks of Payroll 38
   Financial Year 38
   Pay Date 39
   Pay Frequency and Pay Period 39
   The Key Factors Influencing Pay Frequency Across the Globe 40
   Pay Run Classification 41

Statutory Bodies: The Regulatory Framework 43
   Income Tax: A Payroll Essential 43
   Components of Income Tax Calculation 45
   Role of Government Authorities 45
   Impact of Income Tax on Payroll 47

Factors Affecting Income Tax 47
Challenges in Income Tax Calculation 47
Detailed Process flow of how Income tax data flows 48
Social Security: A Safety Net 48
How Social Security Works 49
Importance of Social Security 49
Key Considerations 50
Tax and Social Security Rate Changes 52
Registration and De-registration 54

Payroll Calendar: A Blueprint for Processing 55
Key Components of a Payroll Calendar 55
Importance of a Payroll Calendar 56
How to Build a Payroll Calendar 56
Sample Payroll Calendar 58
Challenges 59
Best Practices 59

Understanding Payroll Data 61
Employee Master Data 61
Personal Data in Payroll Systems 62
Payroll Data and Employment Information 63
Compensation Data 64
Bank Account Details 66
Employee Status: Active vs. Inactive 67
Data Changes and Their Impact on Payroll 70
Employer Master Data 73
Employee Transactional Data 74
Processed Payroll Data 83
Historical Data 84

Processing Payroll in Excel 88
VLOOKUP: Your Excel Superhero 94
Gross Salary: Before Deductions Take a Bite Out of Your Pay 98
Tax Time: The Numbers Game 100
Social Security: Your Safety Net 102
Total Deductions 103
Net Pay: The Money That Matters 104
Employer Contributions 104

Epilogue 106

The Payroll Pilgrim: A Worldwide Quest

In the dawn of civilization, when humans bartered goods and services, the concept of payment was as simple as the exchange itself. But as societies evolved and economies grew, so did the complexities of compensation.

The ancient Egyptians, with their grand pyramids and intricate bureaucracy, were among the first to grapple with payroll. Scribes, armed with papyrus and reeds, meticulously recorded the labor of workers, laying the groundwork for future payroll systems.

Fast forward to the Roman Empire, where legions marched, and bureaucrats calculated. The Romans formalized payroll, paying soldiers in salt (salarium, the root of the word salary) and bureaucrats in coins. This system, while rudimentary, established the concept of regular compensation.

The Industrial Revolution marked a pivotal moment. Time became money, and the time clock, a mechanical marvel, was born. This led to the rise of hourly wages and piecework systems, transforming payroll into a complex calculation of time and productivity.

In the 19th century, the seeds of modern payroll were sown. The United Kingdom introduced income tax in 1798, a harbinger of the complex tax systems to come. The United States followed suit with its first income tax in 1862, though it would be decades before a permanent income tax was established in 1913.

Meanwhile, the concept of social security was emerging. Germany pioneered social insurance programs in the late 19th century, providing a safety net for workers. The United States followed suit with the Social Security Act of 1935, establishing a system of retirement benefits and unemployment insurance.

These developments paved the way for the modern payroll system, a complex interplay of technology, human expertise, and government regulations. From the papyrus scrolls of ancient Egypt to the cloud-based software of today, payroll has evolved to meet the demands of a changing world. The Payroll Party's Booming... and that's Why You Should Join the party!

Introduction:

The world of global payroll is a vast ocean, churning with opportunity. Every year, millions of payroll jobs set sail across the globe. But navigating these exciting waters can feel overwhelming. That's where The Book of Global Payroll comes in - your personal treasure map to becoming a payroll pro!

Forget dry textbooks! The Book of Global Payroll is a four-volume collection, each packed with gold nuggets of wisdom to help you conquer any payroll challenge. Distilled from 15 years of industry experience and countless conversations with payroll ninjas, these guides will equip you with the knowledge and tools you need to succeed.

Here's a sneak peek at the riches within each volume:

- **Volume 1: The Gateway to Global Payroll** This foundational guide lays the groundwork, teaching you the essential secrets every global payroll pirate needs to know.

- **Volume 2: Payroll Project Management: From Chaos to Champion** - Master the art of launching and steering global payroll projects from stormy seas to smooth sailing. Conquer complex challenges and emerge victorious!

- **Volume 3: Forge Your Payroll Partnerships** - Global payroll is a team sport! This volume equips you with the skills to build strong, collaborative relationships with your payroll providers, ensuring everyone is rowing in the same direction.

- **Volume 4: Global Payroll Operations: Running a Well-Oiled Machine** - Imagine the satisfaction of overseeing a global payroll operation that runs like clockwork. Volume 4 provides the essential tools and strategies to keep your payroll ship running smoothly, delivering its precious cargo on time, every time.

The global payroll and HR tech world is on fire! As of 2022, it's a massive $27.65 billion industry, and analysts predict it'll practically double by 2030, reaching a staggering $61.88 billion. That's some serious growth, faster than your coworker who keeps bringing in those hoverboard prototypes (although those things still haven't figured out the whole traffic light situation).

But unlike hoverboards, payroll isn't some futuristic fad. It's a fundamental necessity. People have always needed to get paid, and that's never going to change. As long as there are jobs and salaries, there will be a need for payroll heroes to ensure everyone gets their hard-earned cash on time and accurately. The Bottom Line:

If you're in your 20s and looking for a career with serious staying power, then payroll is your perfect match. It's a rapidly growing field with tons of opportunities, and let's face it, your job security is practically guaranteed. People will always need to get paid, and that means payroll warriors will always be in demand!

The Future of Payroll:

The payroll world is constantly evolving, with new technologies like automation and blockchain integration changing the game. These advancements bring exciting opportunities for those who embrace these advancements. Imagine streamlining complex tasks with automation or using blockchain to create a more secure and transparent payment system - pretty cool, right?

This is just a glimpse of what the future holds for payroll. Are you ready to join the party?

Will you like What you will do?

So, the money and stability of payroll are looking good, but what about the fun factor? Will you actually like doing it?

Here's the thing: payroll can be incredibly exciting, especially if you're a numbers whiz. Imagine rows and rows of data transforming into well-deserved paychecks for hardworking employees. Pretty cool, right?

But payroll isn't just about numbers. Think of it as a fascinating puzzle with legal twists and global variations. Do you enjoy a good challenge and learning new things? If so, payroll has got you covered. With over 190 countries, each with its own payroll regulations, there's always something new to discover.

Maybe you're more of a "people person" who thrives on helping others. Payroll offers that too! Ensuring everyone gets paid accurately and on time is a vital service that keeps the world running smoothly.

Here's the best part:

No matter your specific role in payroll, from processing specialist to compliance officer to product manager, your work has a real purpose. You're the hero behind the scenes, making sure people get their hard-earned cash. Pretty rewarding, wouldn't you say?

So, are you ready to dive into the world of payroll and see if it sparks joy? Don't worry, we can explore the long-term too. Will payroll still excite you in 5 or 10 years? We'll tackle that question next!

Will Payroll Keep You Hooked for the Long Haul?

Absolutely! Take it from someone who's been in the payroll trenches for over a decade (and still feels young, by the way!). In over a decade of experience in global payroll, I've played a whole bunch of different roles, and let me tell you, it's never boring!

I started by managing payroll vendors, then I jumped into the crazy world of processing paychecks for two countries in completely different time zones (talk about juggling!). From there, I went on to implement payroll systems, which involved jet-setting to 14 countries – think passport stamps and cultural immersion! I even tackled integrating some seriously complex software.

But wait, there's more! I also dabbled in product management for a global payroll platform, then switched gears to become a customer service champion, helping folks navigate the payroll maze. And guess what I'm doing now? Product marketing! Yeah, you could say payroll has taken me on a wild ride, and I'm loving every minute of it.

The point is, payroll isn't just one thing. It's a gateway to a diverse and ever-evolving career. Whether you're a tech whiz, a customer service rockstar, or a marketing maven, there's a payroll path waiting for you. And the best part? You'll never stop learning and growing. New technologies, changing regulations, and fresh challenges keep things exciting, year after year.

The good news is, your journey can be just as dynamic and fulfilling as mine. Buckle up, because the world of payroll awaits!

Internal Payroll vs. Payroll Service Provider

Choosing between working for an internal payroll department or a payroll service provider depends on your career goals and preferred work environment. Here's a breakdown of the key differences:

Roles and Responsibilities:

- **Internal Payroll:** Focuses on core payroll tasks like processing payments, calculating deductions and taxes, and ensuring accuracy for your company's employees. You might also collaborate with a central team for tasks like audits or implementing new systems. Some roles might not be available here, such as pre-sales or external client management.
- **Payroll Service Provider:** Offers a wider range of roles beyond core processing. You could be involved in sales, marketing, pre-sales (explaining the system to potential clients), project management (implementing new systems for clients), or even processing payroll for multiple clients.

Work Environment:
- **Internal Payroll:** Offers a stable, collaborative environment focused on your organization's specific needs. You'll become an expert in the company's payroll system and work closely with colleagues in other departments.
- **Payroll Service Provider:** Provides a fast-paced, dynamic environment with opportunities to wear many hats. You'll work with diverse clients, requiring strong communication and adaptability skills.

Client Focus:
- **Internal Payroll:** The company's employees are your primary clients. You'll ensure their paychecks are accurate and delivered on time.
- **Payroll Service Provider:** External companies are your clients. You'll need to understand their specific payroll needs and tailor your work accordingly.

In essence:
- **Internal Payroll:** Specialized, collaborative, client focus on your own company's employees.
- **Payroll Service Provider:** Diverse, dynamic, client focus on external businesses.

The Beauty of Payroll: A Flexible Career Path!

No matter which path you choose, you'll have access to opportunities for growth and learning. You can even move on to analyst firms after gaining experience in either area. Payroll is a field that keeps things interesting with new challenges, continuous learning, and the satisfaction of ensuring people get paid on time! Here are a few sample roles that a career in Global Payroll can offer:

Job Title	Description
Operations	Be the hero behind the scenes! This role keeps the payroll system running smoothly, making sure everyone gets paid on time and accurately. Imagine the satisfaction of ensuring smooth financial operations.
Sales	Channel your inner salesperson! You'll convince companies that your company's payroll system or service is the perfect fit for them. Think clear presentations, building rapport, and celebrating successful deals.
Pre-Sales	Become a payroll explainer! You'll be the tech whiz who breaks down the payroll system and process for potential clients. Think of yourself as a guide, helping them understand the system and ensuring a smooth transition.
Marketing	Become a payroll champion! You'll create eye-catching content that spreads the word about how awesome your company's payroll system is. Think social media, brochures, and website copywriting.
Product	Calling all tech lovers! This role is about improving your company's payroll system. Imagine using your end user understanding, strategic and payroll knowledge to streamline processes and make the system run like a dream.
Engineering	The brains behind the payroll system! You'll build and maintain the complex software that keeps everything ticking. Think about solving coding challenges and ensuring the system runs smoothly.

Job Title	Description
Product Testing	Become a payroll detective! With a keen eye for detail, you'll hunt down any bugs or glitches hiding in the system. Imagine ensuring a flawless payroll experience for everyone.
Integration	The connection specialist! You'll make sure your company's payroll system plays nicely with other systems. Think of it as a puzzle where you ensure everything works together seamlessly.
Business Analyst	Become a payroll problem-solver! You'll analyze data and figure out how to best use the payroll system to meet everyone's needs. Think creative solutions that make everyone happy.
Implementation	The payroll transformation expert! You'll oversee the implementation of new payroll systems, ensuring a smooth transition for everyone involved. Think project management with a focus on collaboration.
Audit	The payroll Guardian! You'll make sure everything is above board by auditing payroll processes and ensuring compliance with regulations. Think keeping things accurate and on the up-and-up.
Project Management	Become a payroll project leader! You'll manage various payroll projects, keeping the team on track and ensuring deadlines are met. Think strong organizational skills to keep things moving smoothly.

So, are you ready to explore the possibilities within the exciting world of payroll? It's a universe with a lot to offer!

Basics of Payroll Process

Before diving deep, let's get familiar with the basics of any country's payroll. We'll explore three key areas:

1) **Payroll Terminology:** Gotta speak the lingo! We'll unveil common terms like "gross pay," "net pay," and "deductions" so you can navigate payroll conversations with ease.

2) **Stages of Payroll:** This is like a recipe – follow the steps, and everyone gets paid on time! We'll break down the different stages, from gathering data to distributing paychecks.

3) **Building blocks of payroll** This section will introduce key concepts that serve as the foundation for effective payroll management.

4) **Understanding Payroll Data:** Data is the fuel that keeps payroll running. We'll explore the different types of data involved, like employee details, time and attendance records, and more.

By understanding these core concepts, you'll be well-equipped to tackle various payroll scenarios, regardless of your specific role (processing, tech, product, integration, or customer success). This strong foundation will come in handy for solving real-time problems!

This revised version keeps your original structure and emphasizes the importance of understanding the basics for anyone working in payroll

Payroll Terminologies

Understanding payroll terminology is essential for anyone involved in the payroll process, whether you're a payroll professional, HR specialist, or business owner. This glossary provides definitions for key terms related to payroll, covering a wide range of topics from employee data and payroll calculations to system processes and reporting.

By familiarizing yourself with these terms, you'll gain a solid foundation for navigating the complexities of payroll and effectively communicate with payroll professionals.

Let's dive into the world of payroll terminology!

Terminology	Terminology Related To	Terminology Explanation
Employee ID	Data	A unique identifier assigned to each employee within the system to avoid confusion due to potential name duplicates.
Payslip	Report	A detailed report for an employee that breaks down their salary, including earnings, deductions, and net pay. It may also include personal information that can vary by country.
Earning	Data	Any component that adds to an employee's salary, such as base salary, bonus, etc.
Deduction	Data	Any component that reduces an employee's salary, such as income tax, undertime, leave without pay, etc.
One-Time Earning	Data	An earning that is paid only once and won't be repeated in subsequent payrolls, such as a bonus.
One-Time Deduction	Data	A deduction that occurs only once and won't be repeated in subsequent payrolls, such as a loan repayment.
Recurring Earning	Data	An earning that repeats in every payroll until a specified

Terminology	Terminology Related To	Terminology Explanation
		end date is reached, such as base salary or employer's social security contribution.
Recurring Deduction	Data	A deduction that repeats in every payroll period until a specified end date is reached, such as loan repayments or income tax.
Effective Start Date	Data	The date from which a pay element becomes active and is included in the employee's payroll.
Effective End Date	Data	The date by which a pay element becomes inactive and is no longer included in the employee's payroll.
Income Tax	Statutory & Data	A government-mandated tax deducted from an employee's salary and paid to the government. The rules and regulations for calculating this tax are determined by the government.
Social Security	Statutory & Data	A government-mandated program that provides benefits to employees. Both employer and employee may contribute to social security. The rules and regulations for contributions are determined by the government.

Terminology	Terminology Related To	Terminology Explanation
Social Security (SC) Employee Contribution	Statutory & Data	The portion of an employee's salary deducted for social security contributions.
Social Security (SC) Employer Contribution	Statutory & Data	The amount contributed by the employer towards an employee's social security benefits.
Gross Salary	Data	The total amount of earnings before any deductions are applied.
Net Salary	Data	The amount of money deposited into an employee's bank account after all deductions are subtracted from gross salary.
Minimum Wage	Statutory & Data	The lowest legal hourly or salaried wage that an employer can pay an employee. This is determined by the government and may vary by country or region.
Overtime	Data	Hours worked in excess of the standard or contracted work hours. These hours are often compensated at a higher rate.
Undertime/Tardy Time	Data	Time deductions applied for being late or not working the full scheduled hours.
LOP (Loss of Pay)/LWP (Leave Without Pay) Absence Data	Data	Deductions applied to an employee's pay for unapproved leave or lack of sufficient leave balance.

The Gateway to Global Payroll

Terminology	Terminology Related To	Terminology Explanation
Financial Year	Statutory	The fiscal year of a country, which may run from January to December or April to March. This period determines when earnings details must be submitted to the government.
Year End	Statutory	The last month of the financial year, during which specific statutory activities are carried out.
Pay Date	Calendar	The specific date on which employees are paid.
Payroll Calendar	Process	A calendar outlining the most important dates related to payroll processing, such as pay dates and deadlines.
Pay Frequency	Process	How often employees are paid, such as monthly, weekly, etc.
Pay Period	Process	The specific timeframe for which an employee is paid on a designated pay date, such as from the 1st to the 31st or from the 15th to the 15th of a month.
Last Mile Activity	Statutory	Activities related to government-mandated requirements.
HRIS System	System	The central database within an organization that stores all employee information.
Absence System	System	A system used to track employee absences, including leave without pay and the number of days worked.

Terminology	Terminology Related To	Terminology Explanation
Time System	System	A system used to track employee work hours, including overtime, undertime, etc.
Integration	Tech	The process of electronically transferring data from one system to another without manual intervention.
Manual Entry of Input	Input	The process of manually entering data into the payroll system one item at a time.
Upload of Input	Input	Uploading a pre-formatted file containing payroll data in a specific format, such as .xls, .csv, etc.
Error Log	Tech	A file that stores details of
Audit Log	Tech	A record of all changes made to the payroll system, including who made the change, when it was made, and what was modified.
Penny Testing	Process	A testing method used to verify the accuracy of newly developed payroll bank files by sending a small, nominal amount (like 1 USD or 1 RS) using the new payment method.
SIT (System Integration Testing)	Process	A testing phase to ensure that different payroll system components and external systems (like HRIS, time systems) work seamlessly together.

Terminology	Terminology Related To	Terminology Explanation
UAT (User Acceptance Testing)	Process	A testing phase where end-users verify that the payroll system meets their requirements and functions as expected.
Parallel Payroll	Process	A testing phase where payroll is processed simultaneously using both the old and new payroll systems for a specific period to ensure accuracy and identify discrepancies.
Hypercare	Process	A post-implementation support period where the implementation and technical teams are available to assist with any issues or questions related to the new payroll system.
Go Live	Process	The official launch date when the new payroll system becomes operational and replaces the old system.
BAU (Business As Usual)	Process	The normal state of payroll operations after the implementation and testing phases are complete.
ESS (Employee Self Service)	Tech	A portal that allows employees to access and manage their payroll-related information, such as payslips and tax forms.

Terminology	Terminology Related To	Terminology Explanation
MSS (Manager Self Service)	Tech	A portal that allows managers to access and manage payroll-related information for their team members, such as approving leave requests and viewing team payrolls.
Payroll Admin	Tech	The user role responsible for processing payroll within the system.
Variance Analysis	Process/Method	A process of comparing payroll data from different pay periods to identify and investigate any discrepancies or changes.
Checklist	Process/Method	A document outlining the steps and tasks to be completed during the payroll process to ensure accuracy and compliance.
Query Handling	Process	The process of addressing and resolving employee inquiries or issues related to their payroll.
Statutory Reports	Report	Government-mandated reports that must be generated and submitted based on payroll data.
Custom Reports	Report	Reports tailored to specific customer or organizational needs, beyond the standard statutory reports.

Terminology	Terminology Related To	Terminology Explanation
Configuration	Tech	The process of customizing the payroll system to meet the specific requirements of an organization without requiring coding changes.
Customization	Tech	The process of modifying the payroll system's code to meet unique organizational needs that cannot be addressed through configuration alone.
YTD (Year-to-Date)	Data	The accumulated payroll data from the beginning of the year to the current date, used for various calculations and reporting purposes.
13th Month Pay	Process	An additional month's salary paid to employees in certain countries as a bonus or mandated benefit.
Blue Collar Payroll	Input	Payroll for employees in physically demanding occupations, such as manufacturing or construction.
White Collar Payroll	Input	Payroll for employees in professional or administrative roles, such as management, clerical, or strategic positions.
New Hire	Input	Payroll data for employees who have recently joined the organization.

Terminology	Terminology Related To	Terminology Explanation
Leaver	Input	Payroll data for employees who are leaving the organization, including their final pay and any necessary deductions.
Re-Hire	Input	Payroll data for employees who have previously left the organization and are now rehired.
Transfer In	Input	Payroll data for employees transferring from another entity within the organization or from a different country.
Transfer Out	Input	Payroll data for employees leaving the organization to join another entity within the organization or in a different country.
COC (Certificate of Coverage)	Input/Statutory	A document issued by the home country of a transferred employee to the host country, confirming that social security contributions are being made in the home country.
Double Taxation	Input/Statutory	A situation where an employee's income is subject to tax in two different jurisdictions.
GL/JV (General Ledger/Journal Voucher)	Output	An accounting file generated by the payroll system that records payroll transactions for financial reporting purposes.

Terminology	Terminology Related To	Terminology Explanation
Upper Cap	Process/Method	A limit imposed on a specific deduction or earning, preventing it from exceeding a certain amount.
LWD (Last Working Day)	Data	The final day of employment for an employee leaving the organization.
DOJ (Date of Join)	Data	The date when an employee joined the organization.
Direct Debit	Process/Method	An automated payment system where funds are directly withdrawn from a bank account.
File	Output	Data stored in an electronic format, such as .xls, .csv, or .txt, for use in other systems.
Report	Output	Human-readable information generated from the payroll system, often in PDF format, for various purposes.
GL Posting Date	Process	The deadline for submitting payroll data to the general ledger for accounting purposes.

Stages of Payroll

Payroll might seem complex, but it all boils down to three key stages, just like many other processes in life! Understanding these stages ensures everyone gets paid accurately and on time. Here's a breakdown:

- **Stage 1: Gathering the Ingredients (Pre-Payroll):**

    Imagine prepping for a delicious meal. This stage is all about collecting the necessary data, like hours worked, salaries, and any deductions (like taxes) that need to be taken out. Think of it as double-checking everything to ensure a smooth and error-free process down the line.

- **Stage 2: The Processing Powerhouse (Payroll-Processing):**

Now that you have all the ingredients prepped, it's cooking time! This stage is where the magic happens. We calculate gross pay (total earnings before deductions), subtract those deductions to arrive at net pay (the amount that actually goes into your pocket), and generate paychecks or arrange direct deposits. Plus, reports are whipped up for tax authorities and other important purposes.

- **Stage 3: Serving Up the Paychecks (Post-Payroll):**

The meal is served! This final stage involves distributing those well-deserved paychecks (or ensuring direct deposits arrive safely) and making sure all tax reports and payments are filed on time. Think of it as cleaning up the kitchen and making sure everything is accounted for.

Table 1 – Simple comparison of Payroll for easy understanding

What do you want?	Driving to Office	Lunch	Pay Employees
Input	Fuel	Vegetables and Grocery, Gas or Electricity	Pre-Payroll readiness
Processing	Engine & Driving	Cooking	Processing Payroll
Output	Reaching Office	Yummy Lunch	Post Payroll
How? / Options	Flight/Car/Motor Bike etc…	Gas Stove/Electrical Cooking	**Input -** Manual or Integration **Processing -** Excel or **System** Post payroll - Manual or automated
Who?	Driver/ Self	Someone else/ Self	Outsourced/In house
Governance	Checking the Fuel Before starting	Checking the grocery or checking the cooking guide before starting	Pre-Payroll Call Post Payroll learning call
Check Points	Monotonous job with less probability of changes so separate checklist is not needed	If someone have to cook what you like, then give them the cooking instruction	Tailored pre, Processing and Post payroll checklists

The Data Maze: Pre-Payroll

Payroll doesn't happen in a vacuum. Data from various systems and teams contributes to a smooth process. Here are some key players:

- **Absence System:** This system provides details like the number of days worked, leave balances, and unpaid leave days. Think of it as tracking attendance and ensuring that everyone gets paid for the time, they've actually put in.

- **Time System:** This system tracks the hours worked, including regular hours, overtime, and any undertime. Imagine it as a timekeeper, ensuring everyone is compensated accurately for their working hours.

- **HRIS (Human Resource Information System):** This system provides information about new hires, leavers, rehires, and any changes to employee data like salary or personal details. (We'll delve deeper into this in the data chapter.) Think of it as the employee master file, keeping track of who's on board and their relevant information.

- **Expense System:** This system provides details about employee expenses that need to be reimbursed. Imagine it as keeping track of out-of-pocket expenses employees incur for work and ensuring they get reimbursed promptly.

Feeding the Payroll Machine: Uploading the Data

Once the data is collected, it needs to be loaded into the payroll system. There are three main methods:

- **Manual Entry:** Data is entered one by one directly into the payroll system. Think of it as handwriting a grocery list. (This can be time-consuming for large organizations.)

- **File Upload:** A file containing the required data (often in .xls, .csv, or .txt format) is uploaded to the payroll system. Imagine it as uploading a digital grocery list. (This is faster than manual entry but still requires some manual work.)

- **Integration:** Data is automatically transferred from the source system to the payroll system without manual intervention. Imagine it as having a self-filling grocery list as per the pre-planned schedule– efficient and error-free! (This is the preferred method, especially for large organizations.)

The Power of Pre-Payroll Planning

A best practice before processing payroll is to hold a "Pre-Payroll Governance Call." This call helps the payroll team and system administrator understand any upcoming changes in the data compared to the previous payroll run. Here's why it's important:

- **Anticipating Workload:** Knowing if there will be a significant increase in new hires, leavers, or compensation changes helps the team prepare for a potentially higher workload.

- **Proactive Problem-Solving:** Identifying potential issues in advance allows the team to address them before they cause delays or errors.

- As a result of this call, the existing payroll checklist should be updated to include key checkpoints to review both during and after payroll processing.

By understanding the pre-payroll stage and its importance, you gain valuable insight into the foundation of a smooth payroll process. Just like a delicious meal requires careful preparation, an accurate payroll requires gathering the right ingredients (data) efficiently!

Image – Payroll Input Data Flow

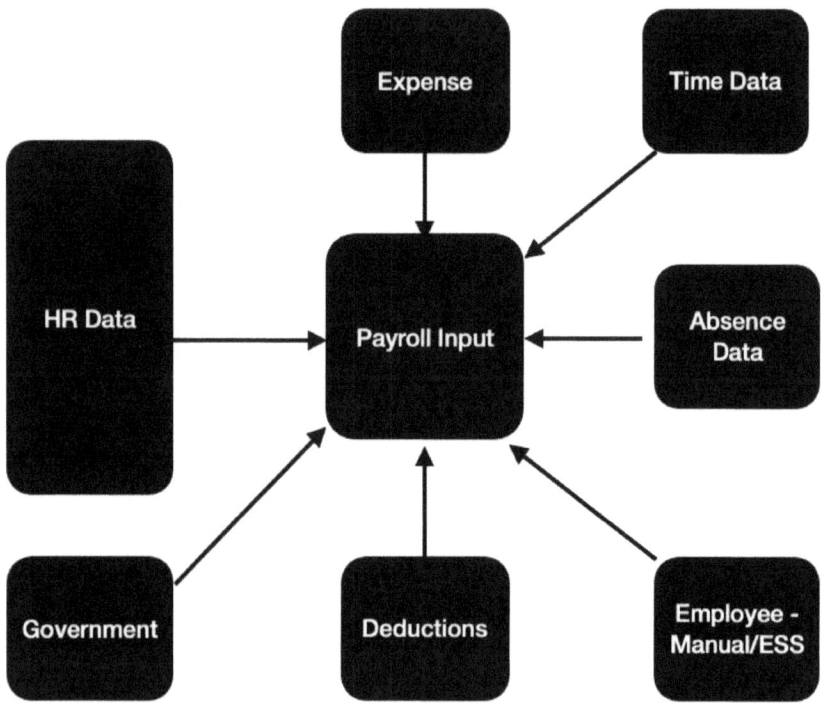

Payroll Processing Stage

Payroll Processing is where the magic happens! This is the stage where all the gathered data is transformed into actual paychecks or direct deposits for employees. Let's break down the key steps involved:

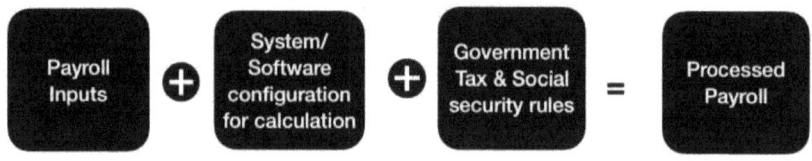

The Payroll Processing Recipe

Payroll Inputs: Think of payroll processing as a high-performance race car speeding toward the finish line. The **Payroll Inputs**—things like hours worked, salaries, allowances, and deductions—are the fuel that powers the engine. Without the right type and amount of fuel, the car simply won't run.

Every piece of data plays a role. The hours logged by employees determine how far the car can go. Salaries and allowances act as the premium-grade additives, ensuring smooth performance. Deductions, like health benefits or loan repayments, are precision adjustments, fine-tuning the output.

But here's the catch: just as a car won't perform with contaminated fuel, payroll processing won't succeed with incomplete or inaccurate inputs. A missed entry or a wrong figure is like pouring the wrong fuel into the tank!

System/Software Configuration for calculation

Picture this: you've just hit the **"Process Payroll"** button. It's like launching a carefully choreographed chain reaction in a sleek, high-tech lab. The payroll inputs—your data about hours worked, bonuses, and other variables—flow into the system, ready to ignite the magic. But what happens next? That's where **System/Software Configuration** takes center stage.

This configuration is the *brains* behind the system, tailored to your company's unique needs. Think of it as the customized blueprint that determines how inputs transform into **Gross Pay**. Every company is different:

- One might have complex overtime rules.
- Another may reward performance bonuses in a specific way.

A third could follow unique leave policies that influence payouts. Each of these variations requires its own configuration—a set of rules and logic programmed into the software to ensure the inputs react exactly as needed when the process begins. It's like a personalized reaction formula: no two companies will have the same settings, even if the basic software is identical. Example – Company A overtime calculation (OT) will be (OT*Basic Pay/hour) *2, whereas company B may have the OT rules as (OT*Basic Pay/hour) *1.5. Informing the system how to handle a certain calculation is called configuration.

Government Tax and Social Security rules-

Every race car, no matter how powerful, needs road signs and regulations to stay on track and cross the finish line safely. In payroll, these Government Tax and Social Security Rules act as the road signs and rules of the road—standardized and universal across all companies operating in the same country.

Once the payroll engine has transformed inputs into **Gross Pay**, these foundational rules kick in. They're like the fixed speed limits or toll booth charges every car must comply with, regardless of who's driving or what car they're using. These rules ensure that taxes are deducted properly, and social security contributions are calculated accurately.

For the employer, this means contributing their share of the costs—like paying a toll as part of the journey. For the employee, it ensures that the system determines the right amount of deductions to arrive at their **Net Pay**—the final destination of the payroll process.

No matter how unique the company's payroll setup is, these standardized rules ensure everyone reaches the finish line on the same road, safely and in compliance with the law.

Processed Payroll:

After all the inputs are processed and the rules are applied, the payroll journey reaches its final checkpoint: **Processed Payroll**. At this stage, the system generates the **Payroll Register**, the first complete output of the entire process.

But just like a race car's performance data is reviewed after crossing the finish line, the Payroll Register undergoes its own checks. Every calculation, deduction, and contribution is validated to ensure accuracy and compliance before finalizing the results.

Validating the Results: Ensuring Accuracy

Once the system churns out the payroll data, it's crucial to verify its accuracy. Here's how it's typically done:

- **Pay Register Review:** The payroll processor manually checks the payroll register, a detailed report listing employee earnings, deductions, and net pay. This can be done in two formats:

Employee-Centric Format: Information for each employee is presented in rows, making it easy to compare details across different pay elements.

Employee ID	Basic Pay	Allowance 1	Deductions	Gross Pay	Income Tax	Employee Contribution	Net Pay	Employer Contribution
10067	100	100	10	190	10	10	170	20
14934	200	100	5	295	20	20	255	40

Pay Element-Centric Format: Information is grouped by pay element (like basic pay, deductions, etc.), making it easier to spot anomalies within each category.

Pay Elements	Amount
Employee ID	10067
Basic Pay	100
Allowance 1	100
Deductions	10
Gross Pay	190
Income Tax	10
Employee Contribution	10
Net Pay	170
Employer Contribution	20

Pay Elements	Amount
Employee ID	14934
Basic Pay	200
Allowance 1	100
Deductions	5
Gross Pay	295
Income Tax	20
Employee Contribution	20
Net Pay	255
Employer Contribution	40

- **Automated Checks:** Some payroll systems include built-in checks to detect potential errors, such as missing data or calculation discrepancies. Features like variance analysis, which compares payroll from the previous pay period to the current one, help identify differences in specific elements or employees. Once a variance is identified, a detailed review is conducted to determine the cause of the change. In the coming years, machine learning and AI are expected to simplify this process even further.

- **Multiple Rounds of Review:** If errors are found, the payroll register goes through revision cycles (Draft 1, Draft 2, etc.) until it's accurate. Excessive revisions indicate potential issues with payroll processes or systems.

From Processing to Payment

Once the payroll register is validated and approved, the final step is to distribute the paychecks or initiate direct deposits. The payroll data is also used to generate reports for tax authorities and other internal purposes.

Remember: The goal of this stage is to ensure accurate and timely payment for all employees while maintaining compliance with tax and labor regulations.

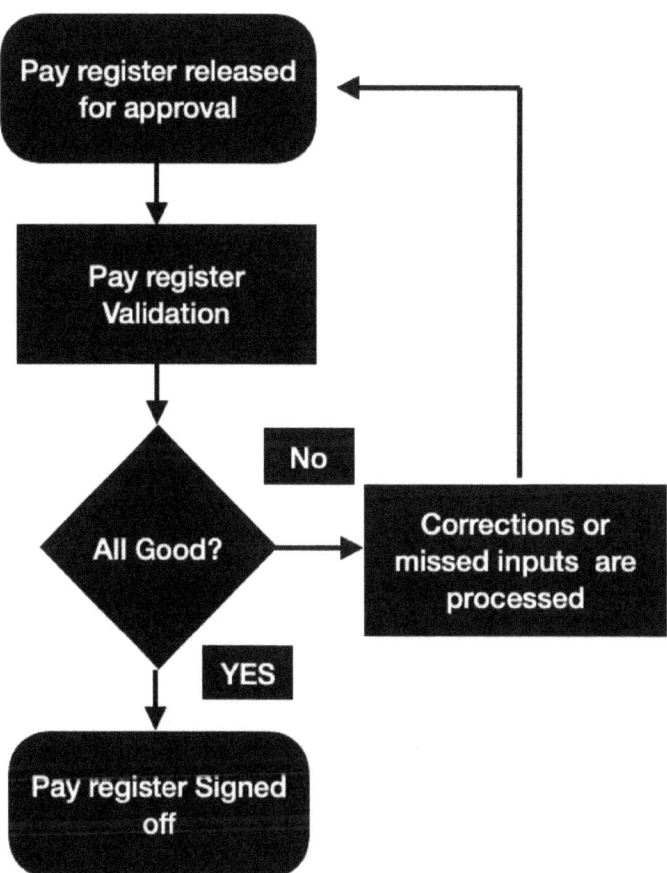

Common Challenges

- **Data Accuracy and Integrity:** Ensuring the accuracy of employee data, time and attendance records, and other inputs is crucial. Errors in this data can lead to incorrect pay calculations.

- **Compliance with Tax and Labor Laws:** Staying updated with constantly changing tax laws, minimum wage regulations, and overtime rules can be complex and time-consuming.

- **System Integration:** Integrating payroll systems with other HR systems (like HRIS, time and attendance) can be challenging and requires careful planning when there is any change that can impact payroll.

Manual Processes: Reliance on manual data entry and calculations can be prone to errors and delays.

- **Employee Input mismatch** – An employee usually needs to provide their information at the time of joining a company or later during their employment when updating personal details. During these processes, there is a significant risk of errors in payroll-impacting information, which can lead to issues such as incorrect net pay calculations or inaccuracies in government contributions. Best Practices

- **Data Validation and Verification:** Implement robust data validation checks to identify and correct errors before payroll processing.

- **Regular System Updates:** Stay updated with the latest tax and labor law changes to ensure compliance.

- **Automation:** Automate repetitive tasks like data entry and calculations to reduce errors and increase efficiency.

- **Employee Self-Service:** Empower employees to access and manage their payroll information through self-service portals, reducing the burden on payroll staff.

- **Regular Audits and Reviews:** Conduct periodic audits to identify and address potential issues in the payroll process.

- **Clear Communication and Documentation:** Maintain clear documentation of payroll processes and procedures for reference and training purposes.

- **Employee Education**: Educate employees on payroll policies and procedures, including how to access their pay information via self-service portals. Emphasize the importance of providing accurate personal information in the system and highlight the potential issues that can arise from incorrect details to raise awareness.

The Post-Payroll Stage

Once the payroll processing is complete and validated, the post-payroll stage kicks in. This phase involves distributing the calculated pay to employees, fulfilling statutory obligations, and generating necessary reports. Let's break it down:

Delivering the Pay

- **Employee Payouts:** The heart of post-payroll is ensuring employees receive their hard-earned money. This is typically done through direct deposit or by distributing physical paychecks.

- **Pay slip Distribution:** Payslips, detailing earnings, deductions, and net pay, are provided to employees either electronically (via email or employee self-service portals) or in paper format.

Fulfilling Statutory Obligations

- **Tax, Social Security and Reports:** Taxes withheld from employee salaries and social security that is withheld and contributed are remitted to the relevant government authorities along with the necessary reports.

- **Compliance Reports:** Other mandatory reports required by government agencies (like labor departments or pension funds) are generated and submitted.

Internal Reporting and Accounting

- **Financial Data:** Payroll data is shared with the finance department for accounting purposes, including generating general ledger entries.

- **Management Reports:** Various reports are created to provide insights into payroll costs, headcount, and other relevant metrics for management decision-making.

In essence, the post-payroll stage focuses on distributing funds to employees, fulfilling legal and regulatory requirements, and providing necessary financial information for the organization.

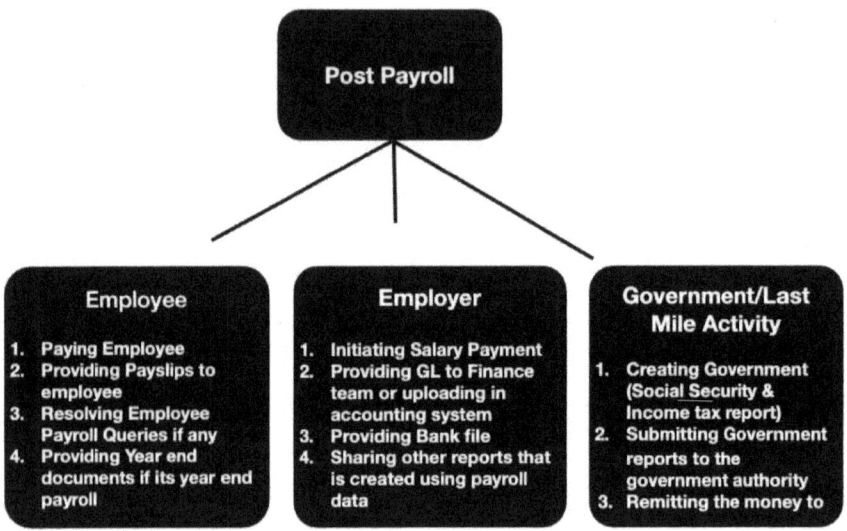

Breaking Down the Post-Payroll Process: Employer's Perspective

The post-payroll stage involves various activities crucial for the organization, including generating necessary files, fulfilling statutory obligations, and ensuring timely payment to employees. Let's explore these key aspects:

Bank File: Enabling Smooth Payments

- **Purpose:** The bank file is a crucial output created after payroll processing to initiate employee payments.

- **Content:** It typically includes employee ID, name, bank account number, SWIFT code, net pay amount, company name, bank account details, and payment date.

- **Format:** Bank file formats vary across different banks (.xls, .csv, .txt, etc.).
- **Process:** The file is uploaded to the bank's portal, approved, and processed. The bank then debits the company's salary account and credits employee accounts.
- **Timeliness:** Timely processing of the bank file is essential to avoid payment delays and potential penalties.

GL File: Feeding the Financial Engine
- **Purpose:** The GL (General Ledger) file provides financial data to the accounting department for recording payroll expenses.
- **Content:** It includes details about salary expenses, tax payments, and other payroll-related costs, categorized by cost centers or departments.
- **Format:** The GL file format depends on the organization's accounting software (e.g., Oracle, SAP).
- **Importance:** Accurate GL files are crucial for financial reporting, budgeting, and decision-making.

Key Considerations
- **Data Accuracy:** Ensuring the accuracy of both bank and GL files is paramount to avoid payment errors and financial discrepancies.
- **Timely Processing:** Timely generation and submission of these files are essential for smooth operations.
- **Security:** Protecting sensitive employee and financial data in these files is crucial.
- **Compliance:** Adhering to banking and accounting regulations is vital.

Post-Payroll: Employee Focus

Once the payroll processing is complete and validated, the focus shifts to ensuring employees receive their pay accurately and on time, along with necessary information.

Pays lips: The Employee's Paycheck Summary

- **Purpose:** Pay slips provide employees with a detailed breakdown of their earnings, deductions, and net pay for a specific pay period.
- **Content:** Typically includes employee details, earnings, deductions, taxes, net pay, and other relevant information.
- **Distribution:** Pay slips are usually distributed electronically (via email or employee self-service portals) or in paper format.
- **Importance:** Pay slips serve as proof of income, are used for tax filing, and help employees understand their earnings and deductions.

Component	Description
Employee Information	Includes employee name, ID, department, and contact details.
Employer Information	Includes company name, address, and tax identification number.
Pay Period	Specifies the dates considered for the payroll.
Gross Pay	Total earnings before deductions.
Earnings	Individual components of an employee's income, such as base salary, allowances, overtime, and bonuses.
Deductions	Amounts subtracted from gross pay, including taxes, social security contributions, loans, and insurance premiums.
Net Pay	The final amount paid to the employee after all deductions.
Year-to-Date (YTD) Totals	Cumulative earnings and deductions for the year.

Component	Description
Tax Information	Details of income tax deductions and other tax-related information.
Bank Account Details	Account number where the net pay is deposited.
Other Information	May include leave balance, loan details, or other relevant information.

Employee Self-Service and Query Resolution

- **Employee Self-Service:** Many organizations provide employees with access to their pay slips and other payroll-related information through online portals. This allows employees to view their pay history, download payslips, and update personal information.

- **Query Resolution:** A robust system for handling employee payroll inquiries is essential. This involves providing clear communication channels and timely responses to employee concerns.

Post-Payroll: The Importance of Employee Query Resolution

The post-payroll phase extends beyond accurate payment and reporting to encompass employee satisfaction and experience. Effective query resolution is paramount to building trust and maintaining a positive employee-employer relationship.

"I have learned that people will forget what you said, people will forget what you did, but people will never forget - How you made them feel" - Maya Angelou. This is the stage where you make an employee feel about their query matters.

Understanding the Critical Role of Query Resolution

- **Employee Satisfaction:** Timely and accurate resolution of payroll inquiries directly impacts employee morale and satisfaction.

- **Organizational Reputation:** How payroll queries are handled reflects the organization's commitment to employee well-being and its overall reputation.
- **Operational Efficiency:** Inefficient query resolution can lead to an increased workload, errors, and a negative impact on productivity.

Query Classification and Resolution

- **Query Levels:** Payroll queries are often categorized into levels based on complexity and required expertise:
  - Level 1: Simple queries that can be resolved through self-service options, FAQs, or automated systems.
  - Level 2: Queries requiring input from payroll subject matter experts or HR representatives.
  - Level 3: Complex queries that necessitate in-depth investigation by payroll specialists.
- **Query Resolution Process:** A well-defined process should be in place to address queries efficiently, including:
  - Acknowledgement of the query
  - Investigation and analysis
  - Communication of findings and resolution
  - Follow-up to ensure employee satisfaction

The Importance of Human Touch

While automation and self-service tools can handle many queries, human interaction remains crucial for complex or sensitive issues. Employees appreciate empathy and understanding when dealing with payroll problems.

Key Considerations for Effective Query Resolution

- **Timely Response:** Employees expect prompt responses to their inquiries.

- **Clear Communication:** Explain the issue and resolution clearly and concisely.

- **Empathy and Understanding:** Show empathy and understanding toward the employee's concerns.

- **Error Prevention:** Analyze query trends to identify and address recurring issues.

- **Employee Feedback:** Seek employee feedback on the query resolution process to identify areas for improvement.

By prioritizing employee query resolution, organizations can enhance employee satisfaction, build trust, and improve overall payroll efficiency.

Common Challenges

- **Timely and Accurate Disbursements:** Ensuring paychecks or direct deposits are delivered on time and with the correct amount can be challenging, especially for large organizations with complex payroll structures.

- **Compliance and Reporting:** Staying updated with ever-changing tax laws and regulations and accurately generating and submitting required reports can be complex and time-consuming.

- **Data Security:** Protecting sensitive employee payroll data from breaches and unauthorized access is crucial.

- **Employee Inquiries:** Handling employee inquiries regarding paychecks, deductions, and other payroll-related issues can be time-consuming.

Best Practices

- **Automated Disbursements:** Utilize direct deposit systems to streamline payment delivery and reduce the risk of errors.

- **Regular Compliance Audits:** Conduct regular audits to ensure adherence to tax and labor regulations.

- **Data Encryption and Security Measures:** Implement robust data security measures to protect employee information.

- **Employee Self-Service Portal:** Provide employees with access to their pay stubs and other payroll-related information through a secure portal.

- **Dedicated Support Channels:** Establish clear channels for employees to inquire about payroll issues and ensure timely responses.

- **Error Prevention and Detection:** Implement processes and controls to minimize errors in payroll data and distribution.

- **Reconciliation and Verification:** Regularly reconcile payroll data with financial records to identify and correct discrepancies.

Building Blocks of Payroll

Understanding the core concepts of payroll is essential for anyone involved in the payroll process. This section will lay the groundwork by exploring fundamental elements that form the backbone of payroll operations. We will delve into key areas such as the financial year, payroll calendar, pay frequency, and statutory regulations.

By the end of this section, you will have a solid grasp of the essential building blocks that underpin payroll processing.

Financial Year

The financial year is a 12-month period used for accounting and tax purposes. It's essential for payroll as it defines the timeframe for calculating earnings, deductions, and tax liabilities.

Key points:

- **Standardized Period:** Provides a consistent basis for financial reporting and planning.

- **Year-End Activities:** Involves tax calculations, reporting, and compliance activities.
- **Tax Adjustments:** Allows for tax refunds or payments based on the calculated tax liability.
- **Country-Specific Variations:** Different countries have different financial year start and end dates.

Pay Date

The pay date is the specific day when employees receive their salary. It's determined by the organization and can vary based on business needs.

Key points:

- **Predetermined schedule:** Pay dates are usually fixed to ensure consistency.
- **Flexibility:** Pay dates can be adjusted, but changes require prior notification to employees.
- **Compliance:** Delayed payments might lead to legal issues.
- **Holiday adjustments:** Pay dates might be shifted if they fall on holidays or weekends.

Pay Frequency and Pay Period

Pay Frequency refers to how often employees receive their salary. Common frequencies include:

- **Weekly:** Employees are paid every week.
- **Bi-weekly:** Employees are paid every two weeks.
- **Semi-monthly:** Employees are paid twice a month, typically on the 1st and 15th or the 15th and the last day of the month.
- **Monthly:** Employees are paid once a month.

Pay Period defines the specific timeframe for which employees are paid. For example, a bi-weekly pay period could be from the 1st to the 15th and the 16th to the last day of the month.

The choice of pay frequency depends on factors like industry, company size, and employee preferences.

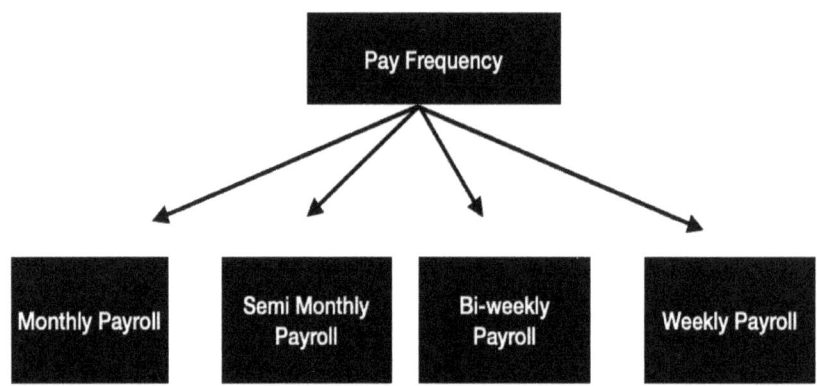

The Key Factors Influencing Pay Frequency Across the Globe

Monthly pay is common in many organizations as it helps reduce the administrative burden of payroll processing, especially in larger corporations, compared to weekly or biweekly cycles. However, several factors influence the decision on pay frequency. Cultural preferences and economic conditions may lead to a preference for biweekly or weekly pay, helping workers manage daily living expenses, particularly in regions where cash flow is critical due to low-income levels. Additionally, labor unions often play a significant role in advocating for specific pay frequencies.

Payroll Period Vs Pay Frequency

Pay Frequency	Monthly	Semi-Monthly	Bi-Weekly	Weekly
Number of Pay Cycle/Number of Pay dates	12	24	26 (Sometimes 27)	52
Difficulty	Less	Medium	Medium	High
Why?	Less expensive when compared to Weekly payroll	Medium Expensive	Medium Expensive	Expensive

Pay Run Classification

In addition to pay frequency and pay period, payroll runs can be further categorized based on different criteria:

Types of Payroll Runs

- **Regular Payroll:** The standard payroll cycle that occurs at the predefined pay frequency.
- **Off-Cycle Payroll:** Payroll runs initiated outside the regular schedule to accommodate specific employee changes or corrections. Sometimes the same is used for paying Bonus payments if the same is not paid with the regular payroll.
- **13th Month Pay:** An additional payroll run to disburse a bonus equivalent to one month's basic salary, common in certain countries

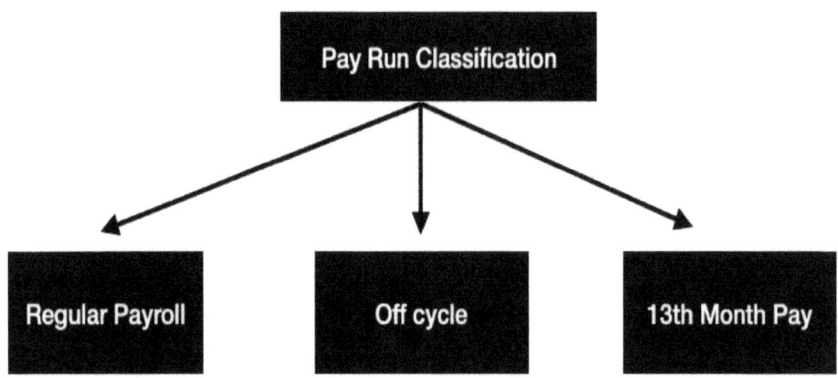

Factors Influencing Pay Run Classification

- **Business Needs:** Organizations may have specific payroll requirements based on their industry, size, and employee composition.

- **Government Regulations:** Statutory obligations and compliance requirements can impact payroll run classifications.

Understanding these classifications helps organizations tailor their payroll processes to meet specific needs and ensure accurate and timely payment to employees.

Statutory Bodies: The Regulatory Framework

Statutory bodies are government entities that establish and enforce laws and regulations governing various aspects of employment, including payroll. Their primary role in payroll is to ensure:

- **Fair and Timely Payment:** Employees receive their wages accurately and on time.
- **Tax Compliance:** Income tax and other statutory deductions are calculated and remitted correctly.
- **Employee Welfare:** Contributions to social security and other welfare schemes are managed appropriately.

By adhering to statutory guidelines, organizations ensure legal compliance and protect the rights of their employees.

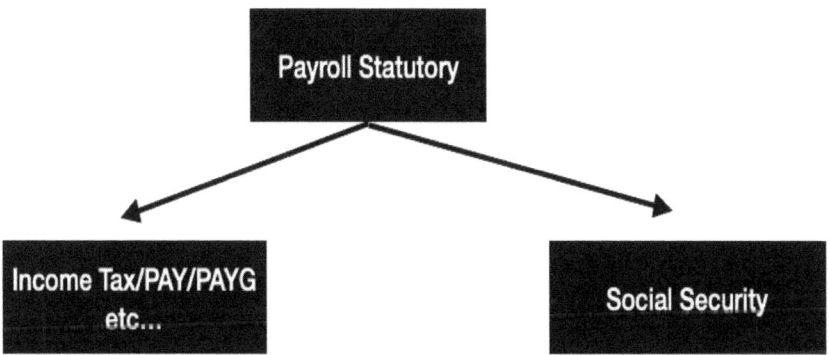

Income Tax: A Payroll Essential

The concept of income tax dates back to ancient Egypt. However, the modern system of income tax as we know it today emerged in the 19th century.

- **Early Forms:** While ancient civilizations-imposed taxes on wealth and property, the taxation of individual income as we understand it today originated much later.
- **Modern Income Tax:** The United Kingdom introduced one of the earliest forms of modern income tax in the early 1800s to fund the Napoleonic Wars. This system laid the foundation for income tax systems in many countries worldwide.

It's important to note that the specific implementation and evolution of income tax vary significantly across different countries, reflecting their economic, social, and political contexts. Income tax is a crucial component of payroll. It's a government-mandated deduction from an employee's salary.

Key points:

- **Employer Responsibility:** Employers are responsible for calculating, deducting, and remitting income tax to the government.
- **Tax-Free Threshold:** Many countries have a tax-free income threshold below which no tax is deducted.
- **Progressive Tax System:** Income tax is often calculated using a progressive tax system, where higher incomes are taxed at higher rates.
- **Tax Slabs:** Income tax rates vary based on income brackets or tax slabs.
- **Government Regulations:** Income tax rules and regulations are determined by the government and can change over time.

Understanding income tax calculations and compliance requirements is essential for accurate payroll processing.

Income tax calculation is a complex process influenced by various factors. Let's break down the key elements involved:

Components of Income Tax Calculation

- **Gross Income:** The total income earned by an individual, including salary, bonuses, rental income, and other sources.

- **Deductions:** Allowable deductions to reduce taxable income, such as standard deductions, Example – In India, investments under Section 80C, and housing rent allowance (HRA).

- **Taxable Income:** The amount of income subject to tax after applying deductions.

- **Tax Slabs:** Different income ranges with corresponding tax rates.

- **Tax Calculation:** Applying the appropriate tax rate to each income slab and summing up the total tax liability.

- **Tax Credits and Rebates:** Adjustments to the calculated tax amount, such as tax credits or rebates offered by the government.

- **Tax Deducted at Source (TDS):** Taxes withheld by employers from employee salaries and remitted to the government.

Role of Government Authorities

- **Tax Regulations:** Governments establish income tax laws, including tax slabs, deductions, and filing requirements.

- **Tax Collection:** Tax authorities are responsible for collecting income tax from individuals and businesses and the method changes from country to country.

- **Compliance Enforcement:** Tax authorities conduct audits and investigations to ensure compliance with tax laws.

- **Deadline:** Income tax deadlines are non-negotiable and missing the deadline results in penalty and below are the few samples by country.

Country	Submission Method	Deadline	Government Authority
India	Electronic submission (Form 24Q)	Monthly or quarterly (based on tax liability)	Income Tax Department (ITD)
United Kingdom (UK)	Electronic submission (Full Payment Submission - FPS)	22nd of the next tax month (monthly) or 22nd day after the quarter ends (quarterly)	HM Revenue and Customs (HMRC)
France	Specialized payroll software	Varies based on company size and payroll frequency	Direction Générale des Finances Pub Liques (DGFiP)
Philippines	Electronic submission through BIR forms (e.g., Form 1702) or online portals	Monthly (10th of the following month) for withholding taxes; Annual income tax return on or before April 15th	Bureau of Internal Revenue (BIR)
Singapore	Electronic submission through my Tax Portal or PAT system	On or before 15th April	Inland Revenue Authority of Singapore (IRAS)

Note: This table provides a simplified overview. Actual procedures and deadlines may vary based on specific circumstances and changes in tax regulations.

Impact of Income Tax on Payroll

- **Payroll Process:** Payroll systems calculate and deduct income tax based on employee information and tax regulations.
- **Year-End Processes:** Payroll departments generate tax-related reports and forms for employees.
- **Compliance:** Adherence to income tax laws is crucial to avoid penalties and legal issues.

Factors Affecting Income Tax

- **Tax Regime:** Different countries have their own income tax systems and regulations.
- **Tax Year:** The period for which income tax is calculated and paid.
- **Residential Status:** An individual's residency status (resident, non-resident, or non-resident Indian) impacts tax liability depending on the country.
- **Age and Dependency:** Age-based exemptions and deductions may apply depending on the country's rules.

Challenges in Income Tax Calculation

- **Complex Tax Laws:** Income tax laws can be intricate and subject to frequent changes.
- **Multiple Income Sources:** Calculating tax for individuals with various income streams can be complex.
- **Deduction and Exemptions:** Understanding eligible deductions and exemptions requires expertise.
- **Advance Tax and Tax Deducted at Source (TDS):** Ensuring compliance with advance tax and TDS requirements.

Detailed Process flow of how Income tax data flows

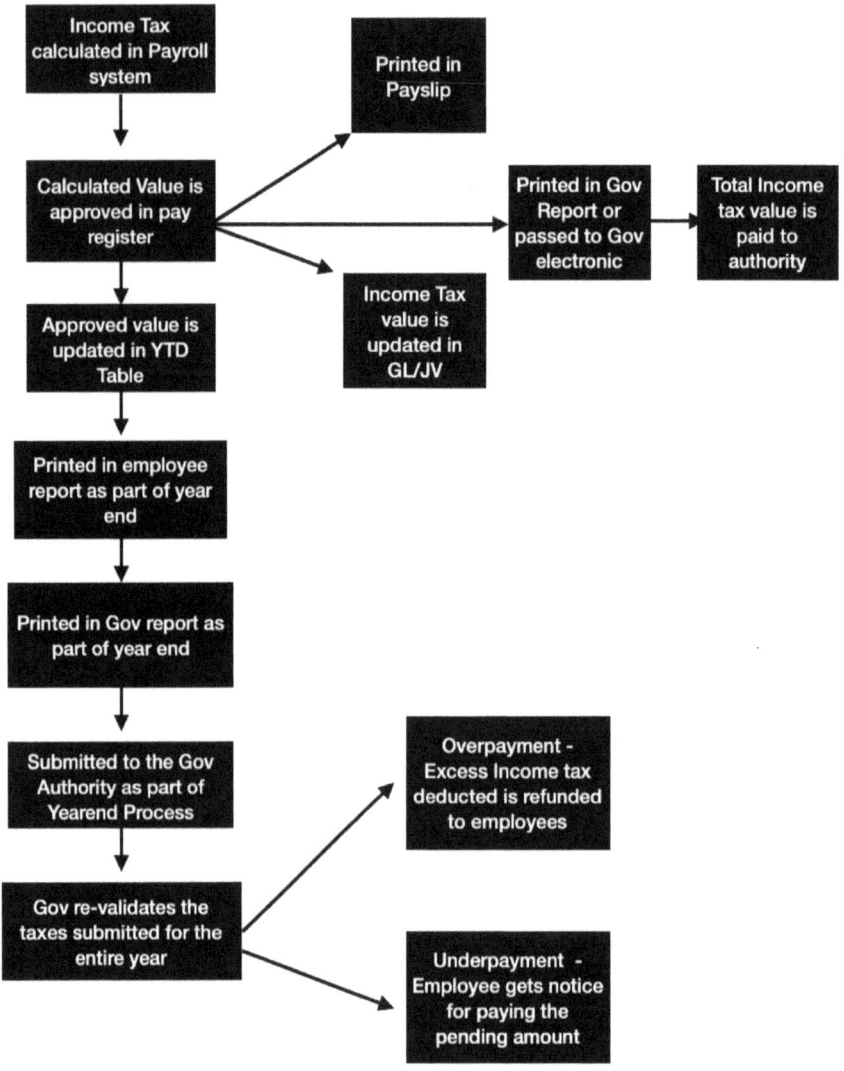

Social Security: A Safety Net

Social security systems are government-mandated programs designed to provide financial protection for individuals and their families in case of retirement, disability, or unemployment.

Key points:

- **Government Oversight:** Social security programs are regulated and administered by government agencies.
- **Employee and Employer Contributions:** Funding typically comes from contributions made by both employees and employers.
- **Benefits:** Social security provides benefits such as retirement pensions, disability payments, and survivors' benefits.
- **Multiple Programs:** Some countries have multiple social security programs covering different aspects of social welfare.

How Social Security Works

- **Employee Contributions:** A portion of an employee's salary is deducted as a social security contribution.
- **Employer Contributions:** Employers also contribute a portion to the social security fund.
- **Fund Management:** Collected contributions are managed by a government agency or a dedicated social security fund.
- **Benefit Eligibility:** Employees become eligible for social security benefits based on factors like age, contribution period, and disability status.

Importance of Social Security

- **Retirement Income:** Provides a financial cushion during retirement.
- **Disability Benefits:** Offers support in case of work-related or non-work-related disabilities.
- **Survivors' Benefits:** Provides financial assistance to families in case of the death of a breadwinner.
- **Healthcare Coverage:** In some countries, social security includes healthcare benefits.

Key Considerations

- **Contribution Rates:** The percentage of salary contributed to social security varies by country and program.

- **Contribution Caps:** There might be maximum income levels subject to social security contributions.

- **Benefit Calculations:** Social security benefits are calculated based on factors such as contribution history and average earnings.

- **Government Oversight:** Social security programs are regulated and monitored by government agencies.

By understanding the mechanics of social security, payroll professionals can ensure accurate deductions and remittances while informing employees about their contributions and potential benefits. Every country has its own.

Country	System Name	Key Components	Contribution Rates (General)
Germany	Sozialversicherungssystem	Pension, health, unemployment, long-term care	Progressive rates based on income for employees and employers
Singapore	Central Provident Fund (CPF)	Retirement savings, housing, healthcare, education	Mandatory contributions from employees and employers (varying rates)
India	Employees' Provident Fund (EPF), Employees' State Insurance (ESI), National Pension System (NPS)	Retirement savings, medical insurance, pension, disability benefits	Varies based on salary and scheme
Philippines	Social Security System (SSS)	Retirement, disability, death, and maternity benefits	Progressive rates based on employee's monthly salary credit
Mexico	Instituto Mexicano del Seguro Social (IMSS)	Healthcare, pension, disability insurance, maternity benefits	Progressive rates based on employee's salary

Note: This table provides a simplified overview. Actual procedures may vary based on specific circumstances and changes in tax regulations.

Social Security Identification number

To effectively manage social security contributions and benefits, unique identification numbers are assigned to both employees and employers. This also varies from country to country and below are few example

Country	Employee Identification Number	Employer Identification Number
Germany	Sozialversicherungsnummer (SV-Nummer)	Employer identification number (Steuer-Identifikationsnummer)
Singapore	Central Provident Fund (CPF) number	Unique Entity Number (UEN)
India	Universal Account Number (UAN)	Employer's Identification Number (EIN)
Philippines	Social Security System (SSS) number	Employer's Registration Number (ERN)
Mexico	Social Security Number (Número de Seguridad Social - NSS)	Taxpayer Identification Number (RFC)

Key Points:

- These identification numbers are crucial for tracking contributions, benefits, and compliance.
- Employers are responsible for registering employees and obtaining their respective identification numbers.
- Governments maintain databases to track contributions and eligibility for benefits.

Tax and Social Security Rate Changes

Tax and social security rates are subject to change over time due to various economic and political factors. These changes can significantly impact payroll processing.

Key Points

- **Regular Review:** Payroll departments must regularly monitor tax and social security rate changes to ensure compliance.
- **Advance Notice:** Governments typically provide advance notice of rate changes to allow for system adjustments.
- **Payroll System Updates:** Payroll software may require updates to accommodate new rates and calculation methodologies.
- **Employee Communication:** Employees should be informed about rate changes and their impact on their take-home pay.
- **Potential Challenges:** Frequent changes can increase the complexity of payroll processing and require additional resources.

By staying informed about tax and social security rate changes, payroll professionals can ensure accurate calculations and avoid compliance issues.

Challenges

- **System Updates:** Payroll software needs to be updated to reflect the new rates and calculation methodologies.
- **Employee Communication:** Employees need to be informed about the impact of rate changes on their take-home pay well in advance for them to pay their financials.
- **Compliance:** Ensuring adherence to new tax and social security regulations can be complex.

Best Practices

- **Regular Monitoring:** Stay updated on tax and social security rate changes through government notifications and professional resources.
- **System Testing:** Thoroughly test payroll software updates to prevent errors and ensure accurate calculations.
- **Employee Communication:** Clearly communicate rate changes and their implications to employees.

- **Documentation:** Maintain detailed records of rate changes and implementation steps.

Registration and De-registration

Registration and de-registration are crucial processes for maintaining accurate records of employees and employers within the social security and tax systems.

Key Points

- **Employee Registration:** Assigning a unique identification number (e.g., UAN, SSN) to an employee and linking them to their employer for tax and social security purposes.

- **Employer Registration:** Obtaining a tax identification number or employer registration number for the organization.

- **Timely Registration:** Ensuring timely registration to avoid penalties and ensure accurate contribution tracking.

- **De-registration:** Removing an employee from the employer's records and updating the relevant government databases upon termination of employment.

Payroll Calendar: A Blueprint for Processing

A payroll calendar is a crucial tool for organizing and managing the payroll process. It outlines key dates, deadlines, and activities throughout the year. Payroll being a time sensitive process, it is very important to make sure Payroll calendar is defined well, maintained and communicated in advance.

Key Components of a Payroll Calendar

- **Pay Periods:** Defines the specific timeframe for which employees are paid (e.g., weekly, bi-weekly, monthly).

- **Pay Dates:** Specifies the exact dates when employees receive their salaries.

- **Cut-off Dates:** Deadlines for submitting employee time and attendance data.

- **Processing Deadlines:** Internal deadlines for payroll calculations and data validation.

- **Payment Deadlines:** Deadlines for transferring salaries to employee accounts.

- **Statutory Compliance Deadlines:** Dates for submitting tax and social security contributions.

- **Year-End Activities:** Includes activities related to tax calculations, reporting, and compliance.

- **Holidays and Non-Working Days:** Accounts for holidays and non-working days that may impact payroll processing.

Importance of a Payroll Calendar

- **Efficiency:** Ensures smooth and timely payroll processing by outlining key activities and deadlines.
- **Compliance:** Helps meet statutory requirements and avoid penalties.
- **Planning:** Enables effective resource allocation and planning for payroll activities.
- **Communication:** Provides a clear reference point for employees, managers, and other departments.

How to Build a Payroll Calendar

1. Define Pay Frequency and Pay Periods:

- Determine the desired pay frequency (weekly, bi-weekly, semi-monthly, or monthly).
- Establish clear pay periods based on the chosen frequency.

2. Identify Key Dates:

- **Pay Dates:** Determine the specific dates when employees will receive their salaries.
- **Cut-off Dates:** Set deadlines for collecting time and attendance data.
- **Processing Deadlines:** Allocate time for payroll calculations, data verification, and report generation.
- **Payment Deadlines:** Establish deadlines for transferring salaries to employee accounts.
- **Statutory Compliance Deadlines:** Determine due dates for tax and social security contributions.
- **Year-End Activities:** Schedule tasks related to year-end processing, such as tax calculations and reporting.

3. Consider Holidays and Non-Working Days:

- Identify holidays and non-working days that may impact payroll processing.
- Adjust pay dates and deadlines accordingly if necessary.

4. Incorporate Statutory Requirements:

- Ensure compliance with tax, labor, and social security regulations.
- Allocate specific timeframes for statutory reporting and compliance activities.

5. Review and Approval:

- Share the payroll calendar with relevant stakeholders (HR, finance, management) for review and approval.
- Incorporate feedback and make necessary adjustments.

6. Communication and Distribution:

- Communicate the payroll calendar to employees, managers, and other relevant departments.
- Distribute the calendar in a clear and accessible format.

Sample Payroll Calendar

Tasks	Tasks Related to	Jan	Feb
Payroll Input Cut off	Payroll Processing	10th	11th
Pay register Draft 1 Sign off	Payroll Processing	15th	16th
Pay register Feedback	Payroll Processing	17th	18th
Final Pay register release date	Payroll Processing	18th	19th
Bank File generated and validated	Employee Payment	20th	21st
Bank File import and approval in Bank Portal	Employee Payment	24th	24th
Employee Salary Payment	Employee Payment	25th	25th
Payslip Dispatch Date	Employee Payment/ Compliance	26th	26th
GL file release	Accounting	27th	27th
GL file import in Finance system	Accounting	28th	28th
Custom Report Release Date	Internal Reporting	24th	24th
Income Tax Report filing	Compliance	10th next month	10th next month
Income Tax remittance	Compliance	10th next month	10th next month
Social Security report filing	Compliance	10th next month	10th next month
Social security Remittance	Compliance	10th next month	10th next month

Remember to adapt this template based on your organization's specific requirements and payroll processes.

By following these steps and creating a comprehensive payroll calendar, you can streamline payroll operations, improve accuracy, and ensure timely payment to employees.

Challenges

- **Dynamic Business Environment:** Changes in staffing levels, employee turnover, and business operations can necessitate adjustments to the payroll calendar.

- **Statutory and Regulatory Changes:** Modifications in tax laws, labor regulations, and social security rules may require calendar updates.

- **System Constraints:** Limitations of payroll software or other systems can impact the flexibility of the payroll calendar.

- **Holiday Variations:** Different holidays across regions or countries can complicate calendar planning.

- **Natural Disasters and Emergencies:** Unexpected events can disrupt the payroll calendar and require adjustments.

- **Communication and Coordination:** Ensuring effective communication and coordination among departments involved in payroll processing is essential.

Best Practices

- **Flexibility and Adaptability:** Build flexibility into the payroll calendar to accommodate changes in business operations, staffing, and regulations.

- **Regular Review and Updates:** Conduct periodic reviews of the payroll calendar to ensure it aligns with current business needs and legal requirements.

- **Communication and Collaboration:** Foster effective communication and collaboration between payroll, HR, finance, and other departments involved in the payroll process.
- **Technology Utilization:** Leverage payroll software and automation tools to streamline calendar management and reduce errors.

Contingency Planning: Develop contingency plans for unexpected events or disruptions that may impact the payroll calendar.

- **Continuous Improvement:** Regularly assess the payroll calendar's effectiveness and identify opportunities for improvement.

Understanding Payroll Data

Payroll data forms the backbone of the entire payroll process. To effectively manage payroll, it's crucial to understand the various components and their interconnections. By categorizing payroll data, we can gain insights into how information flows and influences payroll calculations and outputs.

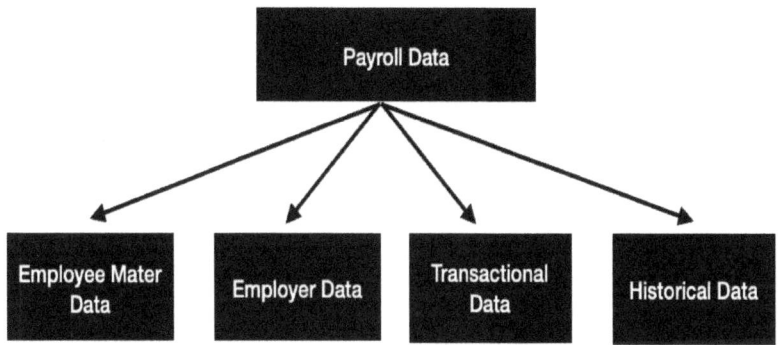

Employee Master Data

Employee master data encompasses all the essential information about an employee required for payroll processing and other HR functions. This data forms the foundation for accurate calculations, reporting, and compliance.

Key Components of Employee Master Data:

- **Personal Information:** Name, date of birth, gender, marital status, contact details, etc.
- **Employment Details:** Job title, department, location, hire date, termination date, etc.
- **Compensation Information:** Base salary, allowances, commissions, bonuses, and other earnings.
- **Bank Account Details:** For direct deposit of salaries.

Personal Data in Payroll Systems

Personal data plays a crucial role in payroll processing and various post-payroll activities. This information must be collected, maintained accurately, and used responsibly.

Types of Personal Data in Payroll:

- **Identification:** Name, date of birth, gender, marital status, and national identification numbers (e.g., PAN, Social Security number).

- **Contact Information:** Address, phone number, and email address.

- **Dependents:** Information used for calculating tax deductions or benefits in certain countries.

- **Bank Account Details:** Necessary for direct salary deposits.

Uses of Personal Data in Payroll:

- **Payroll Calculations:** Dependents' information may impact tax deductions in some countries.

- **Employee Payments:** Bank details are used for secure salary transfers via electronic bank files.

- **Reporting:** National IDs like tax identification numbers and social security numbers are required for tax and other statutory reports.

Data Source and Management:

- Usually provided by employees during onboarding and submitted to the HR team.

- Stored securely in HRIS (Human Resource Information System) or payroll systems.

- Organizations have a responsibility to ensure data privacy and adhere to relevant regulations.

Important Considerations:

- **Data Security:** Implement robust security measures to protect sensitive personal data.

- **Data Minimization:** Only collect and store information essential for payroll purposes.

- **Employee Consent:** Obtain consent from employees for collecting and using personal data and this will be taken care at the time of onboarding an employee

- **Data Accuracy:** Maintain accurate and updated personal data in the system.

Example:

In Japan, a resident taxpayer's deduction for dependents over 16 years old depends on their income and age. Payroll systems in Japan must capture such personal data to calculate accurate tax deductions for employees.

Fun Fact: Organizations take bank information seriously due to potential errors in salary deposits. Verification procedures like requesting a canceled check or double-checking details help prevent accidental payments to incorrect accounts.

Additional Notes:

- Data validation processes are crucial to ensure the accuracy of personal data.

- Regulations around data privacy (e.g., GDPR in Europe) may impose specific requirements on how personal data is collected, stored, and used.

Payroll Data and Employment Information

Employment details encompass information related to an employee's job role, tenure, and employment status. This data is essential for accurate payroll processing, benefits administration, and workforce management.

Key Components of Employment Details:
- **Job Information:** Job title, department, location, job level, and reporting manager.
- **Employment Status:** Full-time, part-time, contract, temporary, or permanent.
- **Employment Dates:** Hire date, termination date (if applicable), and leave of absence periods.
- **Work Schedule:** Regular work hours, shift patterns, overtime eligibility, and leave accruals.
- **Compensation Structure:** Base salary, hourly rate, commission structure, or other forms of pay.
- **Benefits Eligibility:** Entitlement to various benefits based on employment status, tenure, or job role.

Data Sources:
- **HRIS (Human Resource Information System):** Typically, the primary source of employment data.
- **Recruitment Systems:** For new hires and their employment terms.

Compensation Data

Compensation data encompasses the fixed and variable components of an employee's remuneration package. It's crucial for accurate payroll calculations and benefits administration.

Fixed Salary
- **Definition:** A predetermined, consistent amount paid to an employee regardless of performance or other variables.
- **Components:** Typically includes base salary, allowances, and other regular payments.
- **Calculation:** Divided into monthly or weekly amounts based on the payroll frequency.

- **Rounding:** Payroll systems should follow specific rounding rules to avoid discrepancies.
- Example... Employee 16092, Basic Pay 1,20,000/Year. However, a payroll system may need the same as monthly value if it's a monthly payroll or Weekly if it's a weekly payroll. To arrive the same following multipliers are used.
- Yearly to Monthly conversion - Yearly Value /12 = 1,20,000/12 = 10,000/month
- Yearly to weekly conversation - Yearly Value/52 = 1,20,000/52 = 2307.96/week
- Tip - Round off in Payroll is very important and this need to be aligned with the client whether it's going to be two digit, or three digits round off and also whether round up is allowed. Round down should not be done as that may impact the salary that was promised to an employee.

Variable Pay
- **Definition:** Compensation that fluctuates based on performance, organizational goals, or other predefined metrics.
- **Examples:** Commissions, bonuses, incentives, and profit-sharing.
- **Payroll Processing:** Often treated as one-time payments or separate from regular payroll.
- **Data Input:** Requires additional input from departments responsible for performance evaluation or other relevant factors.

Benefits
- **Definition:** Non-cash compensation provided to employees, often with tax advantages.
- **Examples:** Health insurance, retirement plans, meal vouchers, and transportation allowances.
- **Payroll Processing:** May require specific calculations and reporting, depending on the benefit type and tax regulations.

Bank Account Details

Bank account details are essential for disbursing employee salaries through direct deposit. This information is crucial for ensuring timely and accurate payments.

Key Components of Bank Account Details

- **Account Holder Name:** The employee's name as it appears on the bank account.
- **Account Number:** The unique identifier for the employee's bank account.
- **Bank Name:** The name of the bank where the account is held.
- **Branch Details:** The branch name, address, and code (if applicable).
- **Account Type:** Savings or checking account.
- **IFSC Code or Routing Number:** Bank-specific codes for identifying the bank and branch.

Common Challenges

- **Employee Turnover:** Employees frequently change banks or accounts, requiring updates to payroll records.
- **Data Entry Errors:** Incorrectly entered bank account details can lead to payment failures.
- **Bank Account Closures:** Employees may close their accounts without notifying the employer.
- **Data Security:** Protecting sensitive bank account information from unauthorized access and breaches.
- **Bank Account Changes:** Employees may change their bank accounts without informing the employer.

Best Practices

- **Employee Verification:** Implement procedures to verify bank account details upon hire and periodically thereafter.

- **Data Validation:** Use data validation rules to check the accuracy of bank account information.
- **Change Management:** Establish processes for updating bank account details when employees change banks or accounts.
- **Data Security:** Protect bank account information through encryption, access controls, and regular security audits.
- **Employee Communication:** Educate employees about the importance of maintaining accurate bank account information.

Employee Status: Active vs. Inactive

An employee's status within an organization is a critical factor in payroll processing. Understanding the difference between active and inactive employees is essential for accurate payroll calculations and reporting. This section will explore the implications of employee status on payroll operations.

Active vs. Inactive Employees

An essential aspect of employee master data is the distinction between active and inactive employees. This classification determines whether an employee is included in the payroll process.

Active Employees
- **Definition:** Employees currently employed by the organization and receiving regular pay.
- **Payroll Processing:** Included in the payroll cycle for salary calculation, tax deductions, and benefit contributions.

Inactive Employees
- **Definition:** Employees who are no longer actively employed by the organization, either due to termination, resignation, or extended leave of absence.

- **Payroll Processing:** Excluded from the regular payroll cycle. However, certain payroll-related activities might continue, such as final pay calculations, tax filings, and benefit terminations.

Status Changes or Data Changes in Employee Data

While active and inactive statuses determine whether payroll should be processed, other statuses or stages in employee data help manage different types of payrolls. These statuses or data changes could include updates such as promotions, department transfers, or changes in employment type (e.g., from part-time to full-time). Each change may impact payroll calculations, benefits, and other HR processes, ensuring that payroll accurately reflects the employee's current situation.

New Hire

Processing the payroll for a new hire involves different parameters compared to an already active payroll record. For instance, new hires often require proration, and in countries like Hong Kong, new hires begin contributing to social security only after 60 days from their date of joining. Classifying an employee as a new hire also triggers the activation of the ESS portal and other workflows, such as providing their tax and social security number details.

In some systems, re-hires (employees who have rejoined the organization) are also tagged as new hires because proration and other processes remain the same. Similarly, employees who transfer in can also be tagged as new hires.

Key aspects of new hire payroll:

- **Prorated Salaries:** Salaries are often adjusted based on the hire date to reflect the actual number of days worked in the first pay period.
- **Benefit Enrollment:** New hires typically undergo a benefits enrollment process, impacting deductions and payroll calculations.
- **Tax Setup:** Establishing correct tax withholding and filing status based on employee information.

Leaver

An employee's lifecycle status is changed to "Leaver" after their last working day in the organization. These are the employees who have received their full and final settlement. This process ensures that all dues owed to the employee, such as bonus pay and leave encashment, are paid out, with nothing kept on hold.

What is leave encashment?

Depending on company policy, employees can accumulate unused leave during a financial year. These accumulated leaves can then be encashed at the time of leaving as part of the full and final settlement.

Key Components of Leaver Payroll

- **Final Pay Calculations:** Calculating the employee's salary for the final pay period.

- **Leave Encashment:** Calculating the monetary value of unused leaves based on company policy.

- **Gratuity or Severance Pay:** Determining eligibility and calculating any applicable payments.

- **Provident Fund and Other Deductions:** Finalizing contributions to retirement and social security schemes.

- **Tax Adjustments:** Calculating any final tax adjustments based on the employee's overall income.

Transfer

Transfers are classified into two forms: Transfer In and Transfer Out and predominantly used when an employee is moving from one country to another for work under the same organization.

- **Transfer In:** An employee joining a new location, department, or legal entity within the organization.

- **Transfer Out:** An employee leaving a specific location, department, or legal entity but remaining employed by the organization.

Example: Let's assume we are processing payroll for India, and an employee is transferred from the Philippines to India. In this scenario, for India, it's a Transfer In record, and for the Philippines, it's a Transfer Out record.

Depending on the company and country policy, once a transfer out is activated, a full and final settlement might also be initiated. However, in some cases, the employee may remain active in the country from which they are transferred out if the organization has agreed to continue paying a certain amount into their home account to keep social security active or if there is a Certificate of Coverage (COC) in place.

Key Considerations for Transfers
- **Payroll Adjustments:** Updating payroll information to reflect the new location, department, or pay structure.
- **Tax Implications:** Considering potential changes in tax jurisdiction and withholdings.
- **Benefit Adjustments:** Modifying benefit enrollment based on the new location or department.
- **Data Updates:** Updating employee master data with the new location, department, or reporting manager information.

Data Changes and Their Impact on Payroll

Data changes refer to modifications in employee information that can affect payroll calculations and processing. These changes require careful handling to ensure accurate payroll outcomes.

Payroll processing becomes more complex with data changes, as every change can impact the payroll.

Examples:
- If an employee adds a dependent in a country where the number of dependents affects their pay, this will create variances when validating payroll after processing.

- A compensation change with backdated effective dates will initiate a new process of arrear calculation.

In some cases, data changes may not have a major impact:

Examples:
- Changing an employee's bank account number will only affect the data in the bank file.
- A change in employee designation will only impact reports like pay slips where the designation is printed.

Types of Data Changes
- **Personal Information Changes:** Updates to name, address, contact details, marital status, or number of dependents.
- **Employment Status Changes:** Active, Inactive, Notice period etc...
- **Compensation Changes:** Adjustments to base salary, allowances, commissions, or bonuses.
- **Tax Status Changes:** Changes in tax filing status, exemptions, or deductions.
- **Benefit Changes:** Enrollment or disenrollment in benefit plans.
- **Bank Account Changes:** Updates to direct deposit information.

All of these changes have downstream impact not only till processing payroll but also in the post payroll reports.

Employee Master Data Tree

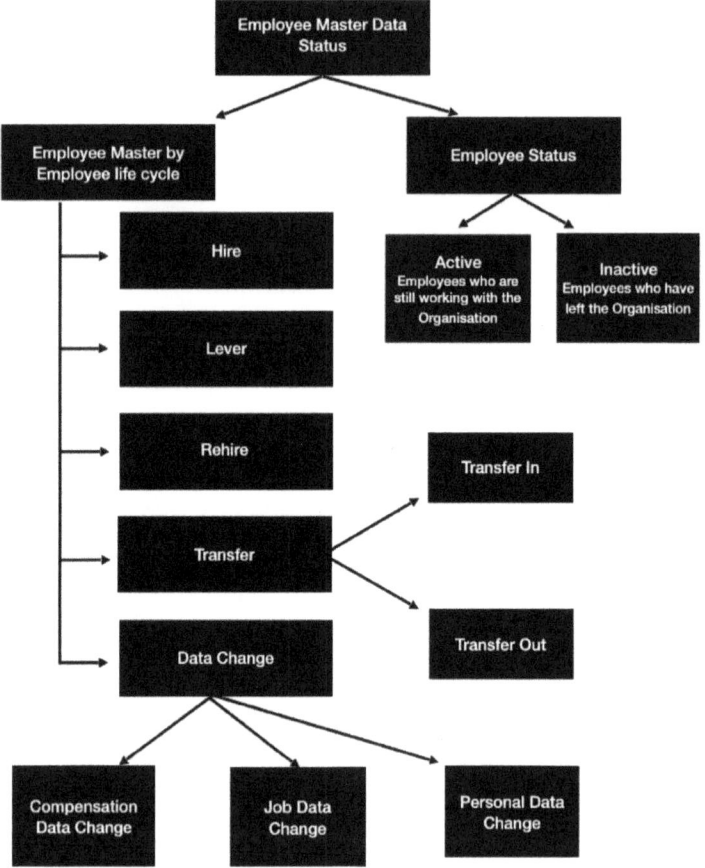

Frequency of Employee Master Data Changes

Employee master data, while relatively stable compared to transactional data, undergoes changes over time. Understanding the frequency of these changes is crucial for effective data management and payroll processing.

Examples:

- **Personal Data:** Changes are rare, usually only when related to name or dependents. For instance, changing your name is not a frequent and mass occurrence.

- **Bank Account:** An employee might change their bank account, but this rarely happens more than twice a year due to the complexity of managing bank accounts.

- **Job Data:** Changes such as band, grade, or designation typically occur once a year, as promotions are not a daily event.

- **Compensation Data:** Often changes only once a year during appraisals or salary negotiations.

While the frequency of master data changes varies, it's generally less frequent as compared to transactional data like time and attendance.

Employer Master Data

Employer master data encompasses the essential information about the organization itself, necessary for payroll processing, reporting, and compliance.

Key Components of Employer Master Data:

- **Organization Details:** Legal name, address, contact information, and tax identification numbers.

- **Business Structure:** Organizational hierarchy, departments, and locations.

- **Banking Information:** Bank account details for salary disbursements and tax payments.

- **Tax Information:** Tax registration numbers, tax filing status, and tax exemption details.

- **Statutory Registrations:** Details of registrations with relevant government authorities (e.g., social security, labor department).

- **Payroll Configuration:** Parameters for payroll processing, such as pay frequency, tax calculations, and deductions.

- **Authorizations:** Details of authorized signatories for payroll-related activities.

Employee Transactional Data

Transactional data consists of inputs provided to the payroll system that differ from the master data. Unlike master data, which remains relatively stable, transactional data can change frequently and varies with each pay period. Examples include:

- Time Data
- Absence Data
- One Time Earnings - Bonuses or incentives
- One Time Deductions

This data ensures that payroll calculations accurately reflect the employee's activities and changes during the pay period.

Time Data

Time data is typically used in payroll for blue-collar, hourly, or part-time (casual) employees. These employees are paid based on the number of hours they work or clock in. Time data is also utilized for white-collar professionals, where timesheets are required to track the hours worked on specific projects. This data is then used for billing customers. In scenarios where an individual works on multiple projects, the resource's expenses must be allocated based on the hours spent on each specific project. In such cases, the timesheet feature proves to be extremely useful.

How is time data captured?

1. **Bio Matrix:** Time data is first captured using a biometric device, such as a fingerprint scanner, ID card, or facial recognition.
2. **Time System:** The data is then processed in the time system, which records the number of hours worked, including regular, overtime, and under time hours.
3. **Payroll System:** Finally, the processed data is sent to the payroll system according to specific requirements for payroll processing.

Any of the above physical method is used for capturing the time data. Typically, it is used when entering or leaving the office.

- **In-Time/Log In Time:** When an employee swipes or logs their entry time.
- **Time-Out/Log Time:** When an employee logs their time at the end of the day.
- Some organizations also track break times to determine exact hours worked.

This data is then sent to the time system for processing, usually at midnight after the day's close.

Example:

- Employee ID 100467 has a shift from 8 AM to 4 PM.
- On June 27, 2024, Employee 100467 logs in at 8 AM IST and logs out at 5 PM IST.
- On June 28, 2024, Employee 100467 logs in at 8 AM IST and logs out at 3 PM IST.

In the time system, the data will be stored as follows:

- **Date:** June 27, 2024
  - **In-Time: 8 AM**
  - **Out-Time: 5 PM**
  - **Regular Hours: 8 hours**
  - **Overtime Hours: 1 hour**
- **Date:** June 28, 2024
  - **In-Time: 8 AM**
  - **Out-Time: 3 PM**
  - **Regular Hours: 7 hours**
  - **Under Time Hours: 1 hour**

Time Data storing format example

Date	Regular Hours	Over Time	Total Work Hours	Under Time
27th June 2024	8	1	9	0
28th June 2024	7	0	7	1

Image 16 - Positive and Negative Hours

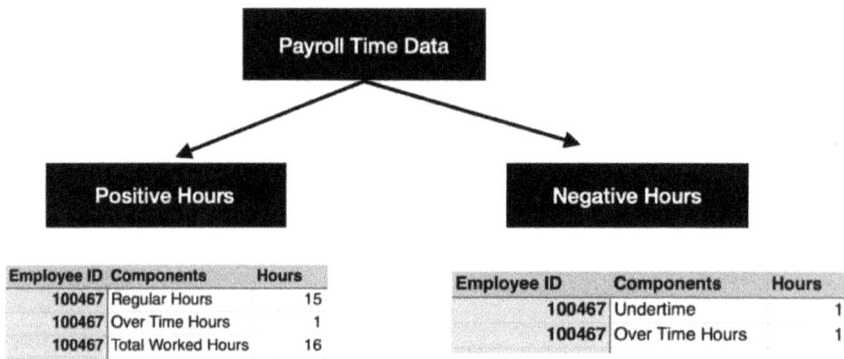

Depending on the payroll system's needs, either the negative hours of under time or positive hours of regular time are sent to the payroll system for payroll processing.

Positive Hours

In this method, the payroll system is sent positive hours for processing payroll (Regular hours worked × Rate) + (Overtime hours ×Rate)\ Negative Hours

In this method, the payroll system only needs the under time (negative hours) and overtime hours: "(Expected working hours ×Rate) (Under-time ×Rate) + (Overtime ×Rate)"

How to Find Per Hour Rate

Assume an employee's annual salary is 120,000, and the expected working hours per day is 8.

Formula -

Step 1 = Salary Per Annum/360* = Per Day Salary => 1,20,000/360 = 333.33/Day

Step 2 = Per Day Salary/8 = Per Hour salary => 333.33/8 = 41.66/Hour

In this example 41.66 is the hourly salary of an employee.

Regular Hours-

These are the hours an employee works according to their regular shift pattern, used for processing payroll.

Example:

- Employee 100467's target working hours are 176 hours (22 days * 8 hours/day).
- If Employee 100467 misses one day, the regular worked hours will be 168 hours (176 hours - 8 hours).

Overtime Hours-

Overtime occurs when an employee works beyond their usual hours.

Example:

- Employee 100467 is supposed to work 8 hours a day / 176 hours a month (8 * 22 days).
- On 2 days, Employee 100467 logs in at 6 AM and logs out at 4 PM = 2 hours overtime.
- On 2 other days, Employee 100467 logs in at 8 AM and logs out at 6 PM = 2 hours overtime.

In this scenario, Employee 100467 has worked 4 hours more than required, and these hours are considered overtime. They are paid at different rates depending on the country's legislation and organizational policy.

Examples of Overtime Rates:

- Night shift overtime: 1.5 times the standard rate.
    - 41.66×1.5
- Regular hours overtime: 1.25 times the standard rate.
- 41.66×1.25=52.08 per hour Working on a holiday like New Year's Day: for this example, let's take 2 times the standard rate.
- 41.66×2=83.32 perhour Complex Overtime Scenarios:
- Working on a holiday with overtime.
- Working night shifts on holidays.
- Working weekends with overtime.
- Combining multiple scenarios, such as holidays that fall on weekends with overtime hours.

The number of days used as a division factor for finding per day salary may change by country law.

It's important to align with the customer/payroll team on how time data will be displayed in the file shared with the payroll team for processing payroll. Whether the time data will be shown as 1.20 (1 hour 20 minutes) or as 1:20.

Every time system captures time differently, and every payroll system has different needs, so it is crucial to align this before starting the project.

An organization can pay more than the government-mandated overtime rate or minimum wage for the hours worked but cannot pay less than government norms.

Absence Data

Absence data plays a crucial role in payroll processing, as it impacts salary calculations and deductions. It encompasses various types of leaves and absences that employees take during their employment.

Key Components of Absence Data

- **Leave Types:** Different types of leaves, such as sick leave, vacation leave, maternity/paternity leave, and unpaid leave.
- **Leave Duration:** Number of days or hours of leave.
- **Leave Dates:** Start and end dates of the leave period.
- **Leave Entitlement:** Accrued leave balances and eligibility for leave types.
- **Leave Approvals:** Approvals from managers or HR
- **Leave Entitlements:** Accrual rules, carryover policies, and maximum leave balances.
- **Absence Requests and Approvals:** Records of leave requests and approval workflows.
- **Absence Periods:** Start and end dates of leave absences.
- **Partial Absences:** Records of half-day or partial absences.

Leave Encashment: Calculating the monetary value of unused leaves upon termination or other specific circumstances where the available leave balance can be converted into salary.

Other Facts

Every organization provides employees with a list of holidays and a leave balance they can use for taking leave. The number of public holidays and minimum leave balance required by law varies from country to country. Some organizations may offer more than the mandatory number of days.

How Payroll system uses Absence Data:

1) **Loss of Pay (LOP) or Leave Without Pay (LWP)**
2) **Leave Encashments**
3) **To Show Leave Balance**
4) **For General Ledger (GL) Entry**

Loss of Pay (LOP) or Leave Without Pay (LWP)

This occurs when an employee applies for leave on a working day that is not approved by the manager or is approved without pay due to insufficient leave balance. This data is used to calculate salary deductions.

Example:

Employee 100467 has 2 days of LWP/LOP.

Step 0 - Find Monthly Salary - 1,20,000/12 = 10,000

Step 1 - Find Per day Salary - 1,20,000/360 = 333.33

Step 2 - Find LOP days - 2 days

Step 3 - Find Value of LOP = LOP Days*Per Day Salary = 2*333.33

= 666.66

Step 4 - Monthly Salary - LOP Salary = 10,000 - 333.33 = 9666.67

This deduction is shown on the pay slip to help employees understand any reduction in salary.

Leave Encashment

Governments mandate a minimum number of leave days an employer must provide. Employers can offer more than this minimum but not less. Leave entitlements accrue over time, and organizations decide how this accrual works. For instance, an employee may earn 1 leave day per month, accruing 0.5 days every 15 days or 1 day after a month. Unused leaves can be encashed or lapse per company policy. To Show Leave Balance

Many countries legally require showing leave balance on payslips so employees can track and plan their leaves. If an organization offers multiple types of leave, the breakdown can be shown on payslips as required by law.

GL File

Leave balances represent a liability for an organization, indicating money owed to employees in the future. This liability is tracked in the GL file for accurate financial accounting.

One-Time Earnings and Deductions

One-time earnings and deductions are non-recurring payments or deductions that impact on an employee's salary for a specific pay period.

One-Time Earnings

- **Definition:** Non-recurring payments made to employees in addition to their regular salary.
- **Examples:** Bonuses, incentives, commissions, reimbursements, and severance pay.
- **Payroll Processing:** Typically treated as separate earning items and added to the regular salary for the pay period.

One-Time Deductions

- **Definition:** Non-recurring deductions made from an employee's salary.
- **Examples:** Loan repayments, damage costs, and other one-off deductions.
- **Payroll Processing:** Subtracted from the employee's gross salary for the specific pay period.

Note: Despite being one-time earnings or deductions, these must be planned in advance and communicated to the payroll team. Processing these elements in payroll software involves several steps:

1. Setting up the pay element
2. Defining calculation rules (e.g., round off, before or after gross)
3. Configuring them in pay slips
4. Configuring them in pay registers and Year-to-Date (YTD) tables
5. Updating GL (General Ledger) codes and rules if necessary
6. Updating details in other reports as required
7. Testing and making changes in a UAT (User Acceptance Testing) environment before moving to production

Recurring Deductions

Recurring deductions are ongoing deductions made from an employee's salary on a regular basis.

Types of Recurring Deductions

- **Statutory Deductions:** Income tax, social security contributions, and other government-mandated deductions.

- **Loan Repayments:** Repayments for loans provided by the employer or external lenders that has to be considered in the Payroll.

- **Advance Salary Recoveries:** Deductions to recover advance salary payments.

- **Court Orders:** Deductions mandated by court orders, such as alimony or child support.

- **Other Voluntary Deductions:** Employee-initiated deductions for investments, insurance premiums, or charitable contributions.

Example Scenario:

Employee 100467 took a loan of 10,000 from the organization, which was paid as a one-time earning in the last payroll. The organization and Employee 100467 agreed to deduct 1,000 every month from the salary for the next 10 months. Here's how the inputs are provided:

Employee ID	Deduction Name	Start Date	End Date	Deduction Amount/Payroll
100467	Company Loan	Jan 2024	Oct 2024	1000

When dealing with one-time or recurring deductions, it's crucial to ensure that these deductions do not reduce an employee's salary below the minimum wage or result in a negative salary. This is essential to comply with legal requirements and to ensure fair compensation for the employees.

In such scenarios, it's important to:

1) **Align with the Customer/HR:** Discuss and agree with the customer (organization) on how deductions should be adjusted to avoid any violation of minimum wage laws or negative salary outcomes.

2) **Adjust Deductions Appropriately:** Make necessary adjustments to deductions before finalizing the pay register. This may involve reducing the deduction amount, spreading out the deduction over a longer period, or exploring other solutions to mitigate the impact on the employee's net pay.

3) **Ensure Compliance:** Verify that all adjustments and deductions adhere to legal regulations and internal policies regarding minimum wage and fair compensation practices.

Processed Payroll Data

Processed payroll data represents the output generated after the payroll calculation and processing phase. This data is essential for various purposes, including employee communication, financial reporting, and compliance.

Key Types of Processed Payroll Data

- **Pay Registers:** Detailed summaries of employee earnings, deductions, and net pay for a specific pay period.

- **Pay slips:** Individualized statements providing employees with a breakdown of their earnings, deductions, and net pay.

- **Year-to-Date (YTD) Reports:** Cumulative earnings, deductions, and tax information for the year.

- **Bank Files:** Electronic files containing payment information for transferring salaries to employee bank accounts.

- **Government Statutory Reports:** Tax-related reports and forms required by government authorities (e.g., tax returns, social security contributions).

- **Custom Reports:** Reports tailored to specific organizational needs, such as headcount reports, labor cost analysis, and payroll metrics.

- **General Ledger (GL) Files:** Data for integrating payroll transactions into the general ledger for financial accounting.

Historical Data

Every country has regulations dictating how long data must be stored in a payroll system by employers and this changes from country to country. Below are few examples-

Country	Minimum Retention Period	Governing Authority
France	5 years	Direction Générale des Finances Publiques (DGFiP)
Mexico	5 years	Secretaría de Hacienda y Crédito Público (SHCP)
India	5 years (minimum), with variations for specific records	Income Tax Department, Ministry of Labour and Employment
Philippines	At least 5 years for tax-related records	Bureau of Internal Revenue (BIR), Department of Labor and Employment (DOLE)
United States	3 years (FLSA), with potential state-specific variations	Department of Labor (DOL)
Canada	3-6 years, depending on province	Provincial labor departments
Brazil	5 years (general), up to 50 years for specific social security records	Ministério do Trabalho e Previdência Social
United Kingdom	No specific statutory requirement, but recommended 6 years	HM Revenue and Customs (HMRC)

Note: These are general guidelines, and actual retention periods may vary based on specific circumstances, industry regulations, and internal policies. It's essential to consult local tax and labor authorities for the most accurate and up-to-date information.

Importance of Historical Payroll Data

- **Compliance:** Adhering to tax, labor, and social security regulations often requires maintaining payroll records for specific periods.

- **Auditing:** Historical data is essential for internal and external audits to verify payroll accuracy and compliance.

- **Reporting:** Generating reports for management, employees, and government agencies requires access to historical data.

- **Analysis:** Analyzing payroll trends, identifying cost patterns, and making data-driven decisions.

- **Dispute Resolution:** Resolving employee inquiries or disputes regarding past earnings or deductions.

Data Retention Requirements

The retention period for payroll data varies depending on:

- **Country-specific regulations:** Labor laws and tax regulations often mandate data retention periods.

- **Industry-specific requirements:** Certain industries may have specific data retention guidelines.

- **Internal policies:** Organizations may establish their own data retention policies based on business needs and risk assessment

Once you understand the difference between Master, Transaction, and processed data and the different types within them life becomes very easy in understanding any countries payroll. This not only helps in processing a payroll but also in designing a payroll system. Project managing Payroll transformation projects and integrating Payroll with complex HRIS and other systems. Now that you have understood the data types in payroll, you will be able to understand any payroll system

The after-credits scene of your payroll journey! Just when you thought the story of *The Gateway to Global Payroll* was wrapping up, here's your surprise twist—practical action! Think of this as your "Suit up, it's hero time" moment.

You've mastered the art of understanding payroll data types—Master, Transaction, processed—and now it's time to roll up your sleeves. We're diving into the *real deal*: **how to process payroll in a spreadsheet**.

I know, spreadsheets don't sound as cool as Iron Man's suit or Thor's hammer. But trust me, armed with the right steps, you'll feel like the payroll equivalent of Captain Marvel—powerful, precise, and unstoppable.

With this guide, you'll confidently tackle any payroll calculation, integrate those numbers like a pro, and emerge with a system so clean and functional that even Nick Fury would give a nod of approval. So, take a deep breath and let's transform that spreadsheet into your payroll superhero cape.

Ready to unlock the step-by-step guide? Let's make those cells come alive!

Harnessing Your Superpower: Manual Payroll Mastery

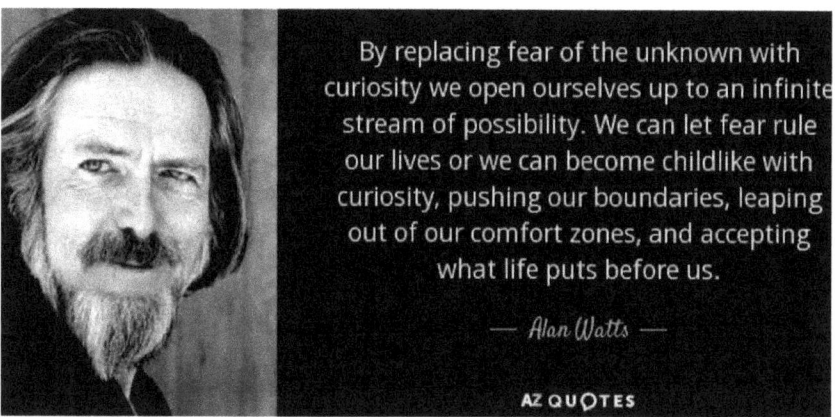

In the age of automation, it might seem counterintuitive to learn how to do something manually. But in the world of payroll, understanding the fundamentals is like knowing the engine of a car. Even if you rely on a mechanic most of the time, it's handy to know how to pop the hood and take a look.

Why bother with manual payroll? Well, for starters, technology, as amazing as it is, can get finicky sometimes. Knowing how to do things the old-fashioned way can be a lifesaver, when the system goes haywire (Worst case).

Beyond that, understanding the mechanics of payroll will give you a deep appreciation for the complexities of the process. It's like learning the magic behind the curtain. You'll see how data flows, how calculations are made, and why certain rules exist.

In this chapter, we're going to roll up our sleeves and get our hands dirty. We'll walk you through the step-by-step process of manual payroll, from data entry to calculations. By the end, you'll have a solid foundation in payroll basics, and you'll be ready to tackle any challenges that come your way.

Processing Payroll in Excel

Step 1: Set the Stage

- Close all those pesky apps cluttering your screen. We want a clean slate for this payroll adventure.
- Open a new Excel workbook and save it as "My Payroll Magic." That's right, we're going to perform some Excel wizardry!

Step 2: Let the Fun Begin

- Follow along as we guide you through the steps. Every time we mention a formula or function, try it out in your own workbook. Don't be afraid to experiment and play around.

Remember: The goal is to have fun while learning. So, roll up your sleeves, grab your keyboard, and let's get this payroll party started!

Step 1: Create a New Workbook

- Open Microsoft Excel.
- Click on "File" -> "New" -> "Blank Workbook."

Step 2: Name Your Master Sheet

Rename the first sheet to "Master Data." This will keep your workbook organized and easy to navigate.

Step 3: Set Up Your Columns

In the first row (starting from cell A1), starting with Employee id like below

The Gateway to Global Payroll

Office on the web Frame	A
1	Employee ID
2	100001

Step 4: Setting up Personal data

Start filling the other column headers as the following. This includes basic information about employees such as -

1. Full name.
2. Date of Birth
3. Hire Date
4. Termination Date
5. Gender
6. Marital Status
7. Nationality
8. National Identification Number

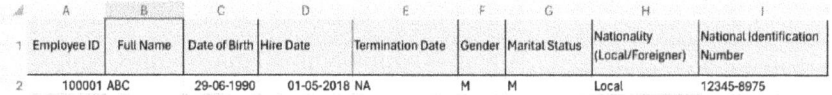

Step 5 – Setting up Employment Details

1. Email address
2. Employment Status
3. Department
4. Job Grade
5. Job Title
6. Part Time/Full Time
7. Work Calendar
8. Pay Frequency
9. Bank Name
10. Branch Code
11. Bank Account Number
12. Bank Beneficial name

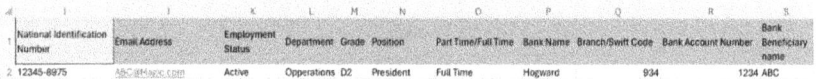

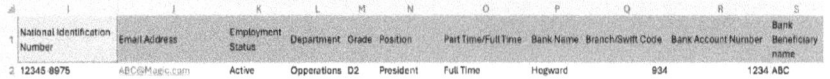

Step 6 - Compensation: The Money Matters

Every company will have its own compensation structure with many components. However, for your learning we will keep it simple and stick with Basic Salary and Fixed allowance 1

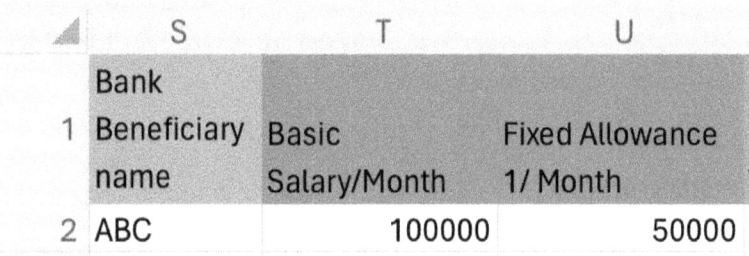

Step 7 - Taxation Details: A Simplified Approach

Taxation is a crucial component of payroll. It ensures that employees contribute their fair share to the government and that the organization complies with tax regulations.

Key Tax-Related Information:

- **Tax Status:** Determines whether an employee is liable to pay income tax. For example, in many countries, foreign employees may have a tax-free period if they stay for less than 180 days.
- **Tax Rate:** The percentage of income that is subject to taxation. This can vary based on tax status, income level, and other factors.

  For our adventure let's keep it simple as Tax status and data as Regular

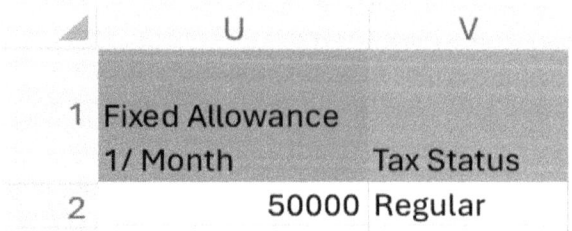

Importance of Updating Master Data:

To ensure accurate payroll calculations, it's essential to keep your master data up to date with any changes in an employee's tax status, dependents, or other relevant information.

Now that we have a solid foundation in master data, let's move on to the next step: creating your input sheet.

Step 8: Creating Your Input Sheet: The Payroll Engine

- Click on the "+" sign next to your "Master Data" sheet to create a new sheet.

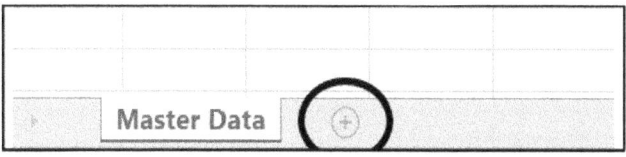

- Double-click the new sheet and rename it "Payroll Input.

- Enter following elements in the sheet Payroll Input
1. Employee Id
2. Full Name
3. Payable Days
4. Variable Allowance 1
5. Over time hours
6. Overt time rate

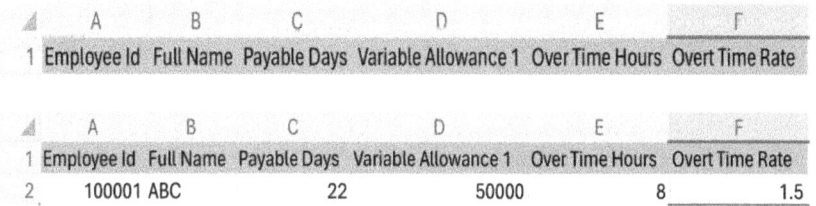

You can start entering values under these headers like shown below

Step 9: Let's set up a simplified tax table for this example.

Create a New Sheet

- Click on the "+" sign next to your "Payroll Input" sheet and name the new sheet "Tax Table."

Define Tax Bracket – Create this simple tax table structure in the sheet "Tax Table"

	A		B
1	Total Wages		Tax rate
2	0	100000	0%
3	100001	150000	10%
4	150001	200000	15%
5	200001	250000	20%
6	250001	300000	25%
7	300001	Above	30%

Defining Social Security

Let us assume social security is going to be strait forward 5% in the gross salary for employee and 10% for employer. Since this is common for all employees, we are not going to create a separate sheet and try to induce these percentages in the formula. In real-world scenarios involving country-specific payroll, you may need to include multiple sheets or sections for social security, as there could be more than one type. For example, the Philippines has three distinct types of social security contributions.

Step 10 - Pay register Creation

Create a new sheet and update the sheet name as "Pay register"

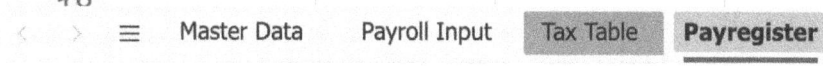

First create the headers for all the earning pay elements from Master data and input sheet like shown in the below picture.

1. Employee Id – Enter all the employee ids you created in Master data file
2. Full Name – We will do – "VLOOKUP" Magic (How to do Vlookup is covered in the next section. Don't worry 😊)
3. Payable Days - Mention "22" as a common number for all employees as we are assuming here, we are only going to pay for 22 days
4. Basic Salary - We will do – "VLOOKUP" Magic
5. Fixed Allowance 1 - We will do – "VLOOKUP" Magic
6. Variable Allowance 1 - We will do – "VLOOKUP" Magic
7. Over Time - We will do – "VLOOKUP" Magic
8. Gross Salary - Excel Magic with formulas we will teach you
9. Income Tax - Excel Magic with formulas we will teach you
10. Employee Contribution - Excel Magic with formulas we will teach you
11. Total Deductions - Excel Magic with formulas we will teach you
12. Net Pay - Excel Magic with formulas we will teach you
13. Employer Contribution - Excel Magic with formulas we will teach you

Copy and paste the employee code from master data to the Pay register sheet and let's start with the Name/First Name.

Before we go to the next step, you need to know about someone called "VLOOKUP"

VLOOKUP: Your Excel Superhero

Imagine VLOOKUP as your personal search engine within Excel. It's a powerful tool that can help you find the information you need fast.

How VLOOKUP Works:

Step 1 - Tell VLOOKUP what to find: Specify the value you want to search for (e.g., employee ID).

Step 2 - Give VLOOKUP a map: Indicate the range of cells where VLOOKUP should search.

Step 3 - Tell VLOOKUP where to look: Specify the column number where you want to find the matching value.

Step 4 - Choose your matching style: Decide whether you want an exact match or an approximate match.

Here's a real-life example

Get employee name and other details by applying "=VLOOKUP" formula in the Pay register. As we have employee Ids in column A and their corresponding salaries in different columns in master data or payroll input. Start with entering the VLOOKUP formula as below

Employee Code	NAME
100001	=VLOOKUP(

Once you enter the formula "=VLOOKUP(A4,'Master Data '!A1:B2,2,FALSE)" you will be able to pull the name of the employee from Master data sheet. If you want to pull the name form Payroll inputs then all you need to do is change the sheet reference and cells reference to the Payroll Input sheet.

Here's how it works:

- **Look up_value**: This is the value you're searching for, which in this case is in cell A1 of the sheet where you want to display the result. For our example, A1 of the pay register is where you'll look.

- **Table_array**: This is the range in the master data sheet where the formula will search for the data. In our example, it's the range from the employee ID column to the Name column, specifically A1 to B2.

- **Col_index_num**: This is the column number within the range that contains the value you want to retrieve. Since we want to return the name, we use 2 because the Name column is the second column in the range.

- **Range_lookup**: This is set to FALSE to ensure the formula finds an exact match.

So, when you apply this formula, it will search for employee ID 100001 in column A of the master data and return the corresponding name from column B, which is ABC.

Basic Salary: The basic salary is a fixed amount agreed upon between the employee and the employer. This calculation is based on the days the employee has worked. The employer needs to record the payable days and calculate the basic salary by converting the monthly salary into a daily rate and then multiplying it by the payable days. You can use VLOOKUP to get the monthly basic salary from the master data, divide it by the standard working days in a month, and multiply the result by the payable days provided by the employer. Refer to the image shown below.

	A	B	C	D
1	Source - Master	Source - Master	Source-Payroll Input	Source- Master & Input - (Formulated Cell)
2				
3	Employee Id	Full Name	Payable Days	Basic Salary
4	100001	ABC	22	=(VLOOKUP(A4,'Master Data'!$A$1:$T$2,20,TRUE)/30)*C4

Fixed Allowances 1: These are like little bonuses on top of your base pay. Think of them as perks to make your job a little sweeter. Just like your basic salary, they're usually tied to the days you work, So, follow the same steps as what you did for basic pay but change the reference (Nidhi to fill and give the same)

Variable Allowances 1: These are the wild cards. They can change from month to month, and they're not tied to your days worked. Think of them as bonuses or incentives. Variable allowances, the amount should be taken from the input sheet, as this is a one-time input and isn't impacted by the payable days.

Remember:

1. The specific rules for calculating these earnings can vary from country to country and company to company. So, make sure you're following the right guidelines.

2. When calculating gross salary, several earnings calculations must be performed. Not all earning pay elements are provided directly by the employer. For example, some pay elements are calculation-based, where you need to derive the amount using the inputs provided and then include it in the gross salary.

Overtime: The Extra Mile

Overtime is like that extra slice of pizza: it's great when you earn it, but it's a whole different story when you have to pay for it.

Formula break-up = ((Monthly Salary / Standard Working Days in a Month) / Standard Working Hours in a Day) * Overtime Hours * Overtime Rate

	A	B	C	D	E	F	G
1	Source - Master	Source - Master	Source-Payroll Input	Source- Master & Input - (Formulated Cell)	Source- Master & Input (Formulated Cell)	Source - Payroll Input	Source - Payroll Input (Formulated cell)
3	Employee Id	Full Name	Payable Days	Basic Salary	Allowance 1	Variable Allowance 1	Over Time
4	100001	ABC	22	73333.33	36666.67	50000.00	=(((VLOOKUP(A4,'Master Data'!$A$1:$T$2,20,TRUE)/30)/8)*1.5)* VLOOKUP(A4,'Payroll Input'!$A$1:$E$2,5,TRUE)

How to Calculate Overtime:

Step 1 - Find hourly rate: Divide your monthly salary by the number of working days and hours in a month.

Step 2 - Tally up those overtime hours: Use VLOOKUP to grab the overtime hours from your input sheet.

Step 3 - Multiply for magic: Multiply your hourly rate by the overtime hours.

Step 4 - Factor in the overtime rate: Check your company's rules. Some places pay double time, others might go for a time-and-a-half rate.

Remember:

- **Overtime in payroll** refers to additional compensation for hours worked beyond the standard workweek or workday.
- Overtime can occur on weekdays, weekends, or public holidays, with rules varying depending on the day.
- Overtime rules or formulas can be specific to the country, company, or outlined in a collective bargaining agreement (CBA).
- Before calculating overtime, ensure the rate complies with labor laws, the CBA, and government regulations, while also aligning with HR policies. Companies can choose to pay more than the government-mandated rate but cannot pay less. For instance, if the government requires 1.5 times the regular pay for night shifts, a company can offer 2 times the pay, but not less than 1.5 times.

Arrears: The Story of Catching Up on Wages

In payroll processing, the term "arrears" might sound a bit formal, but it simply refers to payments made after the usual pay period. Arrears can occur for various reasons, like if timesheets are submitted late, payroll calculations need correcting, or if there's a need to adjust an employee's wages. It's important for employers to keep the communication clear with employees about why there's an arrears payment and to make sure the right amount is paid.

Arrears calculation is a broad topic, so to make it easier, we've split it into two parts: basic and complex. In this chapter, we'll focus on the basics.

Let's take an example to make things clearer. Suppose there's an employee named Krishna whose salary is being processed for February. Krishna's regular monthly salary is Rs. 3000. However, due to an administrative oversight, a Rs. 500 raise that should have been applied starting from January 1st wasn't reflected in his January salary. So, while processing February's salary, we need to include this missed raise. Here's how the arrears would be calculated:

Step 1: Identify the arrear amount.

The arrear amount is simply the difference between what Krishna should have earned and what he actually received. In this case, the arrear amount is the missed raise of Rs. 500.

Step 2: Calculate the arrear payment.

This is the additional amount Krishna should receive to cover the missed raise in January.

Arrear payment = Missed raise = Rs. 500

Step 3: Process the payment.

Since the raise is effective from January 1st, Krishna's February salary will be Rs. 3500, which includes the raise. Now, you add the arrear payment to his February salary.

Total payment for February = Regular salary for February + January arrear payment

**= Rs. 3500 (regular salary) + Rs. 500 (arrear payment)

= Rs. 4000

So, Krishna will receive Rs. 4000 as his salary in February.

Points to Remember:

Arrear calculation depends on the date when the change or scenario occurred.

First, check if the change happened on the 1st of the month or any other date. If it's not the 1st day, the arrear amount will be a combination of the old and new salary rates. We'll dive deeper into this in the next section.

Gross Salary: Before Deductions Take a Bite Out of Your Pay

Once you've calculated all the earnings components, it's time to bring them together.

1. Find the Total: In the last column of your input sheet, use the SUM function to add up all the earnings columns.

Formula Example:

- In cell H4 (assuming your earnings columns are A to I): =SUM(D4:G4)

	A	B	C	D	E	F	G	H
1	Source - Master	Source - Master	Source-Payroll Input	Source- Master & Input - (Formulated Cell)	Source- Master & Input - (Formulated Cell)	Source - Payroll Input	Source - Payroll Input (Formulated cell)	Source = Payregister (Formulated Cell)
3	Employee Id	Full Name	Payable Days	Basic Salary	Allowance 1	Variable Allowance 1	Over Time	Gross Salary
4	100001	ABC	22	73333.33	36666.67	50000.00	5000	165000

Remember -

1. Every country has its own rules for tax-saving components.
2. In India, there's a tax shield of 2,200 rupees for Sodexo (Meal Card).
3. To avoid taxation, this amount should not be included in the Gross salary.
4. It's advisable to create two columns: one for Taxable Gross and another for Non-Taxable Gross.
5. Once all deductions for income tax and social security are calculated from the Taxable Gross, subtract the sum of total deduction amount from the Gross Salary to arrive at the Net Pay.

What are Non-Taxable elements?

These non-taxable elements can include various types of income and benefits that are excluded from taxable income calculations. It's important for both employers and employees to understand these non-taxable amounts to ensure accurate payroll processing and compliance with tax regulations.

Common Examples of Non-Taxable Pay Elements:

- Certain Fringe Benefits
- Gifts and Awards
- Reimbursements for Business Expenses
- Certain Disability Benefits
- Certain Educational Assistance
- Certain Life Insurance Benefits
- Certain Moving Expense Reimbursements

Tax Time: The Numbers Game

Taxes can be a real head-scratcher. But don't worry, we're here to break it down.

Continuing from the previous example of gross salary, let's assume the gross salary is fully taxable, with no non-taxable income to deduct which is 165,000 as per our calculation in the gross section of the book.

The next key factors are **tax rates** and **tax brackets**. The government establishes these to calculate the tax amount. Income tax rates are typically structured into brackets, where different portions of income are taxed at varying rates. Below is an example of a tax table, which illustrates tax rates and brackets:

Total Wages		Tax rate
0	100000	0%
100001	150000	10%
150001	200000	15%
200001	250000	20%
250001	300000	25%
300001	Above	30%

Now that we have the taxable income and tax rates, let's calculate the tax amount, assuming the tax table above represents a progressive tax rate system.

To make this process clear, start by adding columns for each tax bracket. This approach helps to easily identify how each tax bracket is calculated and locate any errors.

	H	I	J	K	L	M	N
1	Source = Payregister (Formulated Cell)	Source = Tax Table & Pay register (Formulated Cell)					
2		Income Tax					
3	Gross Salary	0%	10%	15%	20%	25%	30%

Steps to Calculate Tax Amount:

Step 1: Since the tax rate for income up to 100,000 is 0%, subtract 100,000 from the taxable income (gross salary). i.e., 165000.

- No tax on the first 100,000 of the taxable income = 0
- Taxable Income = 165,000 - 100,000 = 65,000

Step 2: Check the ceiling of the second bracket.

- 2A) If the bracket's ceiling is **lower than** the taxable income, subtract the lower ceiling from the higher ceiling of the bracket and apply the tax rate for that slab. Continue this process until the bracket ceiling exceeds the taxable income.

- 2B) If the bracket ceiling is **higher than** the taxable income, calculate the tax rate on the difference between the taxable income and the lower ceiling of that bracket.

Continuing our calculation - Example:

- Here, 165,000 exceeds the higher bracket ceiling of 150,000.
- Tax on the second bracket: (100,001 - 150,000) * 10% = 4,999.9

Step 3: Since the taxable income (165,000) falls into the third bracket, follow Step 2(b). Subtract the lower range from the taxable salary and apply the tax rate for that slab.

- Tax on the third bracket: (165,000 - 150,000) * 15% = 2,249.85

Step 4: Add the tax amounts from all the steps to calculate the total tax owed for the income earned. i.e. add total income tax column after the 30%

slab column. This is the tax amount you are supposed to pay for the income earned.

H	I	J	K	L	M	N	O
Source = Payregister (Formulated Cell)	Source = Tax Table & Pay register (Formulated Cell)						Formulated Cell
	Income Tax						
Gross Salary	0%	10%	15%	20%	25%	30%	Total Tax
165000	0	4999.9	2249.85	0	0	0	7249.75

- Total Tax Amount = 0 + 4,999.9 + 2,249.85 = 7,249.75

Social Security: Your Safety Net

When thinking about Social Security, it can be viewed as a safety net. In many countries, Social Security contributions are mandatory amounts that are deducted from an employee's paycheck to help fund programs that support retirees, disabled individuals, and the families of those who have passed away. These contributions go towards essential benefits like health insurance, retirement funds, and life insurance.

But Social Security contributions aren't just one-sided; they're a team effort between the employee and the employer. There are also options for voluntary contributions, which might include charitable donations or union dues.

So, how does it all work? **Employee Contributions:** An employee contributes a certain percentage of their wages directly to Social Security. This isn't an extra cost to the employee; it's simply deducted from their gross salary and sent to the government by the employer.

Employer Contributions: The employer also contributes, paying a percentage to Social Security on behalf of the employee. This contribution doesn't reduce the employee's salary; instead, the employer pays it directly to the government. The rates for these contributions can be the same for both the employee and the employer, or they may differ.

Employers need to ensure accurate calculations—not just because it's required by law, but because it directly affects the net pay the employee receives. The amounts deducted are credited to an account in the employee's name with the government, providing a safety net for the future. Additionally, staying updated on tax laws and regulations is essential for compliance.

Let's break it down with an example:

Imagine the Social Security contribution rate for an employee is 5%, and the employer's rate is 10%. The government decides what portion of the salary these percentages apply to—often the gross salary. For this example, let's assume it's based on the gross salary.

- **Employee Contribution:** 5% of 165,000 = 8,250
- **Employer Contribution:** 10% of 165,000 = 16,500

In this way, both the employee and the employer contribute to a system designed to provide financial protection in the long term. In the below screenshot you will see employee contribution but not employer contribution because employer contribution is always shown after Net Pay in pay register. We will touch up on specifically on employer contribution again after Net Pay

Remember - While employee contribution is shown as a deduction on their paychecks, employers make a separate payment to the government on behalf of their employees.

	H	I	J	K	L	M	N	O	P
1	Source = Payregister (Formulated Cell)	Source = Tax Table & Pay register (Formulated Cell)						Formulated Cell	Formulated Cell
2		Income Tax							
3	Gross Salary	0%	10%	15%	20%	25%	30%	Total Tax	Employee Contribution
4	165000	0	4999.9	2249.85	0	0	0	7249.75	8250

Total Deductions

To calculate the net pay, sum up all the deductions and label the cell as "Total Deductions." Using the same example:

- **Total Deductions** = Total Taxes + Employee Social Security Contribution
- **Total Deductions** = 7,249.75 + 8,250

- **Total Deductions** = 15,499.75

Source = Payregister (Formulated Cell)	Source = Tax Table & Pay register (Formulated Cell)						Formulated Cell	Formulated Cell	Formulated Cell
	Income Tax								
Gross Salary	0%	10%	15%	20%	25%	30%	Total Tax	Employee Contribution	Total Deductions
165000	0	4999.9	2249.85	0	0	0	7249.75	8250	15499.75

Net Pay: The Money That Matters

Net pay is the final amount an employee takes home after all deductions are taken out. It's the money that actually shows up in their bank account.

Calculation:

- **Net Pay = Gross Salary - Total Deductions**

Example:

- Gross Salary: ₹165,000
- Total Deductions: ₹15,499.75
- Net Pay: ₹165,000 - ₹15,499.75 = ₹149,500.25

Now, you have the employee's net pay, which is the amount they'll receive.

Employer Contributions

After calculating the Net Pay, it's important to mention the Employer Contributions. Although these amounts are not deducted from the employee's salary, the employer is responsible for paying them to the government on the employee's behalf.

Reminder – Always show employer contributions after the Net Pay so that it does not confuse you and by mistake you don't deduct employer contribution also from Net Pay.

- **Employer Contribution:** 10% of gross salary (₹165,000) = ₹16,500

	O	P	Q	R	S
1	Formulated Cell	Formulated Cell	Formulated Cell	Formulated Cell	Formulated Cell
2					
3	Total Tax	Employee Contribution	Total Deductions	Net Pay	Employer Contribution
4	7249.75	8250	15499.75	149500.25	16500

Did your calculations match the book? If so, you're well on your way to becoming a payroll wizard. If not, don't worry. Even the best of us can make mistakes. The key is to learn from them and keep practicing.

Remember: While Excel is a powerful tool, it's not always the most efficient way to handle payroll. Understanding how to process payroll manually can be a lifesaver in worst-case scenarios, like system downtime or unexpected changes.

So, keep mastering Excel, but don't forget to learn the ins and outs of your payroll system. That way, you'll be prepared for anything.

Epilogue

Congratulations! You've reached the end of this payroll journey, and what a journey it has been! Let's take a moment to reflect on everything you've achieved through this book.

You've gained a solid foundation in the **basics of Global Payroll**, exploring how this billion-dollar industry operates and the exciting career opportunities it offers. In addition to mastering payroll terminologies, data structures, and the various stages of payroll processing, you've also developed a strong understanding of **Global Payroll compliance**, including income tax and social security contributions—essential knowledge for success in this field.

Having processed payroll yourself, you now have the confidence to excel in any role, whether as a Payroll Processor, Implementation Lead, Project Manager, or Product Manager. While every system may vary on the surface, the fundamental principles you've mastered will empower you to thrive in any environment.

We're thrilled to announce that **three more volumes** are on the horizon, diving even deeper into the world of payroll. Stay tuned for more insights, tools, and strategies to advance your expertise!

All the best for your journey ahead in the world of payroll! For any questions or further guidance, feel free to reach out to us at **payrollbook@outlook.com**.

Happy Payrolling!

The Payroll Book Team

www.ingramcontent.com/pod-product-compliance
Lightning Source LLC
LaVergne TN
LVHW061554070526
838199LV00077B/7044